Robert Frost
A Tribute to the Source

ROBERT FROST

A Tribute to the Source

Poems by Robert Frost
Photographs by Dewitt Jones
Text by David Bradley

Holt, Rinehart and Winston 🦋 New York

Text copyright © 1979 by David Bradley
Photographs copyright © 1979 by Dewitt Jones
Published by Holt, Rinehart and Winston,
383 Madison Avenue, New York, New York 10017.
Published simultaneously in Canada by Holt, Rine-
hart and Winston of Canada, Limited.

Library of Congress Cataloging in Publication Data

Frost, Robert, 1874–1963.
    Robert Frost, a tribute to the source.

    1. Frost, Robert, 1874–1963. 2. Poets,
American—20th century—Biography. I. Bradley,
David, 1915–   II. Jones, Dewitt. III. Title
PS3511.R94Z518 1979   811'.9'12 [B] 78–10444
ISBN 0–03–046326–2

Designer: Jon Goodchild
Printed in the United States of America
10 9 8 7 6 5 4 3 2

Frontispiece photograph courtesy the Kathleen
Morrison Collection.

Grateful acknowledgment is made for use of the
following:

Selections from *The Poetry of Robert Frost* edited
by Edward Connery Lathem. Copyright 1916, 1923,
1928, 1930, 1934, 1939, 1947, 1949, © 1969 by Holt,
Rinehart and Winston. Copyright 1936, 1940, 1942,
1944, 1948, 1951, © 1956, 1958, 1962 by Robert Frost.
Copyright © 1964, 1967, 1968, 1970, 1975, 1976,
1977 by Lesley Frost Ballantine. Reprinted by permission of Holt, Rinehart and Winston, Publishers.

Selections from *Interviews with Robert Frost* edited
by Edward Connery Lathem. Copyright © 1966 by
Holt, Rinehart and Winston. Reprinted by permission of Holt, Rinehart and Winston, Publishers.

Passages from Terrence Ortwein's unpublished play,
Swinger of Birches. Copyright © 1977 by Terrence
Ortwein. Reprinted by permission of the author.

To Babs and Lilla

The Gift Outright

The land was ours before we were the land's.
She was our land more than a hundred years
Before we were her people. She was ours
In Massachusetts, in Virginia,
But we were England's, still colonials,
Possessing what we still were unpossessed by,
Possessed by what we now no more possessed.
Something we were withholding made us weak
Until we found out that it was ourselves
We were withholding from our land of living,
And forthwith found salvation in surrender.
Such as we were we gave ourselves outright
(The deed of gift was many deeds of war)
To the land vaguely realizing westward,
But still unstoried, artless, unenhanced,
Such as she was, such as she would become.

Contents

Color photographs appear on pages 23–30, 47–54, 71–78, 95–102, 119–126, and 143–150.

Robert Frost
A Tribute to the Source

1. *Coming*

The land was seabottom before it was land. It was silt and sediment flickering down in sunlit shallows for half a billion years while the oceans took on salt and great sharks coursed among squalls of warmwater fish. The land came up as reefs and islands, growing into long north-south ranges which, weathered 300 million years, became Vermont. Farther to the east under a steaming sea, bubbles of boiling granite surged up through the sediments, cured, and were uncovered in later eons. They formed the coiled mountains of New Hampshire, the barbed coast of Maine.

After that, long after, the ice came down from Labrador, shaping the mountains, piling up the tailings in the valleys. The last ice, in places more than a mile thick, scoured all the peaks and valleys as far south as Nantucket and Long Island, finally bedding down to melt under a world of gray debris, leaving to lichens and moss the job of building soil.

When at last the continent began to warm—some fourteen thousand years ago—the old-stone Indians were already here. Grassland people from the west, hunters of big game, they followed the mastodon and bear, the bison and musk ox. They moved north with the edge of ice, leaving here and there their stone weapons and the charcoal of camps where they had fished and celebrated the return of spring.

Later tribes came to occupy the old sites, but living now where arctic forests had spread across the tundra. More clever with tools, more settled in their camps, they learned to snare small game, stitched clothing, cooked with pottery, built weirs for fish in the rivers. They burned clearings in the forests where they could grow a winter's supply of corn, beans, and squash; they ran trails for trade or war through the mountain notches. For more than thirty thousand seasons this was their land, until the coming of the Europeans.

The first to come were Northmen cruising down the coast of Labrador to Newfoundland, marveling at the stands of timber, so scarce back home in Greenland. They liked what they saw —called it the Miraculous Strands and Vinland the Good—but Eskimos ran them out. Five hundred years later the voyagers began to appear, plowing the gray seas on the wind of a rumor that China and India lay close at hand, just around the next headland or the next after that. In a hundred years of searching they found no passage to Cathay.

But the word was out: not spices—not gold—but cod and whales in numbers unimaginable. Portuguese fishermen, French, Basque, English, left their home ports in late January and beat across the Atlantic in order to be on the Grand Banks for the spring catch. Plain farmers of the sea, they knew a good crop when they saw one. By the time the famous explorers arrived, claiming whole coasts for great kings, fishermen in scores were already settled there and taking their harvests.

All down the coast of foggy Nova Scotia and into the Gulf of Maine, it was the same: miraculous seas. At Smith's Islands—lately called the Isles of Shoals—fishermen worked in double crews, one to fish, the other ashore to split the cod and dry them on the rocks. Standing in stink and gurry, the men could look across to the mainland where the first shacks were going up and banners of smoke were rising over the clearings.

Robert Frost tells of one family

> Whose claim is good to being settled here
> Before the era of colonization,
> And before that of exploration even.
> John Smith remarked them as he coasted by,
> Dangling their legs and fishing off a wharf
> At the Isles of Shoals, and satisfied himself
> They weren't Red Indians but veritable
> Pre-primitives of the white race, dawn people
> Like those who furnished Adam's sons with wives;
> However uninnocent they may have been
> In being there so early in our history.
> They'd been there then a hundred years or more.

Fish and timber brought them, farming settled them. Among the early arrivals was Robert Frost's first American ancestor. Sailing over from Devon in a small bark, he landed at a rivermouth in New Hampshire. Others were there already, so he moved to Kittery, Maine, and took up farming. For the next two hundred years the Frosts remained on this coastal plane. One fought in the Indian wars, one in the Revolution. Cautious farmers, they were unmoved by the pioneers pushing north and west to take up lands in the mountains. Later, when the great tide set across New England, carrying the venturesome to Oregon and California, the Frosts stayed put.

Sand Dunes

Sea waves are green and wet,
But up from where they die
Rise others vaster yet,
And those are brown and dry.

They are the sea made land
To come at the fisher town
And bury in solid sand
The men she could not drown.

She may know cove and cape,
But she does not know mankind
If by any change of shape
She hopes to cut off mind.

Men left her a ship to sink:
They can leave her a hut as well;
And be but more free to think
For the one more cast-off shell.

The Birthplace

Here further up the mountain slope
Than there was ever any hope,
My father built, enclosed a spring,
Strung chains of wall round everything,
Subdued the growth of earth to grass,
And brought our various lives to pass.
A dozen girls and boys we were.
The mountain seemed to like the stir,
And made of us a little while—
With always something in her smile.
Today she wouldn't know our name.
(No girl's, of course, has stayed the same.)
The mountain pushed us off her knees.
And now her lap is full of trees.

A Prayer in Spring

Oh, give us pleasure in the flowers today;
And give us not to think so far away
As the uncertain harvest; keep us here
All simply in the springing of the year.

Oh, give us pleasure in the orchard white,
Like nothing else by day, like ghosts by night;
And make us happy in the happy bees,
The swarm dilating round the perfect trees.

And make us happy in the darting bird
That suddenly above the bees is heard,
The meteor that thrusts in with needle bill,
And off a blossom in mid-air stands still.

For this is love and nothing else is love,
The which it is reserved for God above
To sanctify to what far ends He will,
But which it only needs that we fulfill.

Our Hold on the Planet

We asked for rain. It didn't flash and roar.
It didn't lose its temper at our demand
And blow a gale. It didn't misunderstand
And give us more than our spokesman bargained for;
And just because we owned to a wish for rain,
Send us a flood and bid us be damned and drown.
It gently threw us a glittering shower down.
And when we had taken that into the roots of grain,
It threw us another and then another still,
Till the spongy soil again was natal wet.
We may doubt the just proportion of good to ill.
There is much in nature against us. But we forget:
Take nature altogether since time began,
Including human nature, in peace and war,
And it must be a little more in favor of man,
Say a fraction of one percent at the very least,
Or our number living wouldn't be steadily more,
Our hold on the planet wouldn't have so increased.

Wind goes from farm to farm in wave on wave,
But carries no cry of what is hoped to be.
There may be little or much beyond the grave,
But the strong are saying nothing until they see.

2. Settling

There may have been a beginning but as far as anyone could remember there was never an end to the work. New England hill farmers needed no Boston theocrats to explain God's will: work was salvation, plain enough. For the needs of this day, for next week and next year, men, women, children, horses, had to make do, out of the stony earth and under the changing sky. Yet for two centuries that was enough. The forests supplied timber for buildings, wood for fires, and meat, skins, furs, sugar. The fields—an immense job to clear even with the help of hogs and fire—provided crops and pasturage.

In rain or slop or snow, in spells of muggy heat and clouds of blackflies, in sunshine or sudden frosts, New Englanders lived with the weather and had little time to feel sorry for themselves. They developed a flat laconic speech to moderate the steep hills, and a wry sense of comedy to counter harsh weather.

When the cycle of seasons began anew, crows were the heralds. Some creamy dawn in late February all the crows in the territory would wake up and start shouting. It was time to get things going again—Town Meeting time, sugaring time, mud season. After that, while women turned the winter's grease to soap, men and boys cleared fields, pulled stumps, burnt brush, skidded out stones, built walls. April, May—a hurry to plow, and a prayer for the season ahead:

O, God, if You'll forgive our little jokes on You, . . . we'll forgive Your one great big joke on us. . . . You know what God's great big joke on us is? . . . It begins in delight and ends in we don't know what kind of a crop.

Haying, haying . . . whenever three days permitted, dawn to dark through the longest days, and always an eye to the clouds prowling on the hills. August: mowing, threshing, berries, and the outpourings of the garden. (Once a year only was there such a season for feasting.) Then into harvest time: lay up corn, beans, squash, and root vegetables, for on any night now the white scythe would come to mow the fields. Apples: all the varieties that two hundred years of ingenuity could breed: apples for cider, vinegar, applejack, tubs of apple butter, strings of dried apples for winter pies. At last, November: slaughter month, smoke month, ham, bacon, salt beef, salt pork.

The farm is a base of operations—a stronghold. You can withdraw into yourself there.
"Fill your cellar and fill your larder" so that you can go into the siege of winter with zest.
Go to the cellar stairs; look at the preparations for winter. Smell the apples. Have a good cellar.
That is a part of the good life.

Too soon the day would come when the moist wind thickened, the air congealed to a fine powder, until everything was coming down in long slanting lines across a world grown dim in grays. The men, driven indoors at last, repaired sleighs and wagons, forged plowshares, fixed tools, built buckets and barrels for the year ahead. The women spun flax and wool, wove blankets, made clothes, dipped candles, and prepared the never-ending meals. When the snow was deep enough it would be time for men to go to the forests again to fell trees for next year's building.

No catching up on what had been let go, but a chance the farm might be half ready when the crows came round with spring again.

Unlike the conquistadores in the south, burning for gold, or the French in Canada, trading for furs, these English had come for land. Where better for a second son to go, or the dispossessed from the lordly estates of England? Land meant freedom, a kind of freedom unknown in Europe. It meant the right to be oneself, "all the risks taken," including the risk of "going to hell in [one's] own way."

Beyond self-reliance and a mechanical ingenuity picked up in the shops of the Midlands, the colonists brought an instinct for self-government learned from their Viking conquerors five hundred years earlier. They also came with a profound suspicion of large ruling systems of any kind: kings, nobles, armies, archbishops.

There is a good deal of God in everything [we] do. . . . I'd be afraid, though, of any one
religion being the whole thing in one country, because there would probably come a day when
they would take me down to the cellar and torture me—just for my own good.

It was a strong society that settled the isolated valleys of New England. It kept its privacies behind stone walls but stitched itself together with town roads and town government. When the upheaval of revolution came, New Englanders had had two hundred years of experience with self-government. It seemed only natural for Vermonters to declare and establish their own free republic, for New Hampshire people (with the help of John Adams) to write the first state constitution.

Church on Sundays, school in winter, provided the continuities, while farming brought the good things in life. Where all were farmers, there was work but no drudgery. Where there were children and horses there was entertainment aplenty, and stories for the neighbor passing on the road or met beside a cider barrel. Births, weddings, deaths—times for remembering, times for renewal. At harvest time the fiddlers came to lead the rejoicing; in winter the air was alive with the sound of sleigh bells; on July Fourth, the ringing of church bells, fire bells, school bells, welled up through the green valleys and was answered across the hills by farm bells announcing pride and hope and jubilation over land and independence.

All this was more than a hundred and fifty years ago.

After 1830 the ebb set in. Deep soil in the West, California gold, and then the Civil War wasted New England farms. Vermont and New Hampshire sent thousands of young men to the war; after it was over, fewer than half wanted to return to the old hill ways. In the seasons that followed, railroads crawled up into the back country; mills went up where there was water power; scattered villages clustered into riverside towns and small cities. The farms, once so hand-fashioned and independent, were gradually shaped to a money economy, caught in a web of dependence upon the cities.

For a while Spanish sheep and winter lumbering preserved the farms, but then in the 1870s and '80s the girls danced off to the cities—Lowell, Lawrence, Manchester—where there were jobs and money. Vermont farmers turned downhill to dairying, New Hampshire to chickens, and the puckerbrush took back the hills.

> Let those possess the land, and only those,
> Who love it with a love so strong and stupid
> That they may be abused and taken advantage of
> And made fun of by business, law, and art;
> They still hang on. . . .

Who but the poets tell of the lives of people? County courts file deeds of ownership, church records and family Bibles imperfectly describe the successions, but only the poets—dawdlers, visionaries that they are—hear our ancestors talking.

The traveler in New England today can scarcely imagine these hills as they were, more than half in open fields and pastures, and farmed right up to the abutments of the great mountains. Let him stray but a little way into any forest and he will come upon a blue-gray wall built of blocks so large he will swear that only a race of giants could have piled them up so. It is a modern fossil, the backbone of a vanished civilization.

Or let him climb a high ridge and of a sudden, in the midst of a hardwood tangle, he will find his hat snatched off and himself taken by the thousand fingers of some arthritic old apple tree. He will hear a shiver of welcome in its leaves, will feel in its clutch a stubborn life that just won't let go.

The Vanishing Red

He is said to have been the last Red Man
In Acton. And the Miller is said to have laughed—
If you like to call such a sound a laugh.
But he gave no one else a laugher's license.
For he turned suddenly grave as if to say,
"Whose business—if I take it on myself,
Whose business—but why talk round the barn?—
When it's just that I hold with getting a thing done with."

You can't get back and see it as he saw it.
It's too long a story to go into now.
You'd have to have been there and lived it.
Then you wouldn't have looked on it as just a matter
Of who began it between the two races.

Some guttural exclamation of surprise
The Red Man gave in poking about the mill,
Over the great big thumping, shuffling millstone,
Disgusted the Miller physically as coming
From one who had no right to be heard from.

"Come, John," he said, "you want to see the wheel pit?"

He took him down below a cramping rafter,
And showed him, through a manhole in the floor,
The water in desperate straits like frantic fish,
Salmon and sturgeon, lashing with their tails.
Then he shut down the trap door with a ring in it
That jangled even above the general noise,
And came upstairs alone—and gave that laugh,
And said something to a man with a meal sack
That the man with the meal sack didn't catch—then.
Oh, yes, he showed John the wheel pit all right.

The Runaway

Once when the snow of the year was beginning to fall,
We stopped by a mountain pasture to say, "Whose colt?"
A little Morgan had one forefoot on the wall,
The other curled at his breast. He dipped his head
And snorted at us. And then he had to bolt.
We heard the miniature thunder where he fled,
And we saw him, or thought we saw him, dim and gray,
Like a shadow against the curtain of falling flakes.
"I think the little fellow's afraid of the snow.
He isn't winter-broken. It isn't play
With the little fellow at all. He's running away.
I doubt if even his mother could tell him, 'Sakes,
It's only weather.' He'd think she didn't know!
Where is his mother? He can't be out alone."
And now he comes again with clatter of stone,
And mounts the wall again with whited eyes
And all his tail that isn't hair up straight.
He shudders his coat as if to throw off flies.
"Whoever it is that leaves him out so late,
When other creatures have gone to stall and bin,
Ought to be told to come and take him in."

Mowing

There was never a sound beside the wood but one,
And that was my long scythe whispering to the ground.
What was it it whispered? I knew not well myself;
Perhaps it was something about the heat of the sun,
Something, perhaps, about the lack of sound—
And that was why it whispered and did not speak.
It was no dream of the gift of idle hours,
Or easy gold at the hand of fay or elf:
Anything more than the truth would have seemed too weak
To the earnest love that laid the swale in rows,
Not without feeble-pointed spikes of flowers
(Pale orchises), and scared a bright green snake.
The fact is the sweetest dream that labor knows.
My long scythe whispered and left the hay to make.

The Code

There were three in the meadow by the brook
Gathering up windrows, piling cocks of hay,
With an eye always lifted toward the west
Where an irregular sun-bordered cloud
Darkly advanced with a perpetual dagger
Flickering across its bosom. Suddenly
One helper, thrusting pitchfork in the ground,
Marched himself off the field and home. One stayed.
The town-bred farmer failed to understand.

"What is there wrong?"

              "Something you just now said."

"What did I say?"

          "About our taking pains."

"To cock the hay?—because it's going to shower?
I said that more than half an hour ago.
I said it to myself as much as you."

"You didn't know. But James is one big fool.
He thought you meant to find fault with his work.
That's what the average farmer would have meant.
James would take time, of course, to chew it over
Before he acted: he's just got round to act."

"He *is* a fool if that's the way he takes me."

"Don't let it bother you. You've found out something.
The hand that knows his business won't be told
To do work better or faster—those two things.
I'm as particular as anyone:
Most likely I'd have served you just the same.
But I know you don't understand our ways.
You were just talking what was in your mind,
What was in all our minds, and you weren't hinting.
Tell you a story of what happened once:

I was up here in Salem, at a man's
Named Sanders, with a gang of four or five
Doing the haying. No one liked the boss.
He was one of the kind sports call a spider,
All wiry arms and legs that spread out wavy
From a humped body nigh as big's a biscuit.
But work! that man could work, especially
If by so doing he could get more work
Out of his hired help. I'm not denying
He was hard on himself. I couldn't find
That he kept any hours—not for himself.
Daylight and lantern-light were one to him:
I've heard him pounding in the barn all night.
But what he liked was someone to encourage.
Them that he couldn't lead he'd get behind
And drive, the way you can, you know, in mowing—
Keep at their heels and threaten to mow their legs off.
I'd seen about enough of his bulling tricks
(We call that bulling). I'd been watching him.
So when he paired off with me in the hayfield
To load the load, thinks I, Look out for trouble.
I built the load and topped it off; old Sanders
Combed it down with a rake and says, 'O.K.'
Everything went well till we reached the barn
With a big jag to empty in a bay.
You understand that meant the easy job
For the man up on top, of throwing *down*
The hay and rolling it off wholesale,
Where on a mow it would have been slow lifting.
You wouldn't think a fellow'd need much urging
Under those circumstances, would you now?
But the old fool seizes his fork in both hands,
And looking up bewhiskered out of the pit,
Shouts like an army captain, 'Let her come!'
Thinks I, D'ye mean it? 'What was that you said?'
I asked out loud, so's there'd be no mistake,
'Did you say, "Let her come"?' 'Yes, let her come.'
He said it over, but he said it softer.
Never you say a thing like that to a man,
Not if he values what he is. God, I'd as soon
Murdered him as left out his middle name.
I'd built the load and knew right where to find it.
Two or three forkfuls I picked lightly round for
Like meditating, and then I just dug in

And dumped the rackful on him in ten lots.
I looked over the side once in the dust
And caught sight of him treading-water-like,
Keeping his head above. 'Damn ye,' I says,
'That gets ye!' He squeaked like a squeezed rat.
That was the last I saw or heard of him.
I cleaned the rack and drove out to cool off.
As I sat mopping hayseed from my neck,
And sort of waiting to be asked about it,
One of the boys sings out, 'Where's the old man?'
'I left him in the barn under the hay.
If ye want him, ye can go and dig him out.'
They realized from the way I swabbed my neck
More than was needed, something must be up.
They headed for the barn; I stayed where I was.
They told me afterward. First they forked hay,
A lot of it, out into the barn floor.
Nothing! They listened for him. Not a rustle.
I guess they thought I'd spiked him in the temple
Before I buried him, or I couldn't have managed.
They excavated more. 'Go keep his wife
Out of the barn.' Someone looked in a window,
And curse me if he wasn't in the kitchen
Slumped way down in a chair, with both his feet
Against the stove, the hottest day that summer.
He looked so clean disgusted from behind
There was no one that dared to stir him up,
Or let him know that he was being looked at.
Apparently I hadn't buried him
(I may have knocked him down); but my just trying
To bury him had hurt his dignity.
He had gone to the house so's not to meet me.
He kept away from us all afternoon.
We tended to his hay. We saw him out
After a while picking peas in his garden:
He couldn't keep away from doing something."

"Weren't you relieved to find he wasn't dead?"

"No! and yet I don't know—it's hard to say.
I went about to kill him fair enough."

"You took an awkward way. Did he discharge you?"

"Discharge me? No! He knew I did just right."

October

O hushed October morning mild,
Thy leaves have ripened to the fall;
Tomorrow's wind, if it be wild,
Should waste them all.
The crows above the forest call;
Tomorrow they may form and go.
O hushed October morning mild,
Begin the hours of this day slow.
Make the day seem to us less brief.
Hearts not averse to being beguiled,
Beguile us in the way you know.
Release one leaf at break of day;
At noon release another leaf;
One from our trees, one far away.
Retard the sun with gentle mist;
Enchant the land with amethyst.
Slow, slow!
For the grapes' sake, if they were all,
Whose leaves already are burnt with frost,
Whose clustered fruit must else be lost—
For the grapes' sake along the wall.

The Black Cottage

We chanced in passing by that afternoon
To catch it in a sort of special picture
Among tar-banded ancient cherry trees,
Set well back from the road in rank lodged grass,
The little cottage we were speaking of,
A front with just a door between two windows,
Fresh painted by the shower a velvet black.
We paused, the minister and I, to look.
He made as if to hold it at arm's length
Or put the leaves aside that framed it in.
"Pretty," he said. "Come in. No one will care."
The path was a vague parting in the grass
That led us to a weathered windowsill.
We pressed our faces to the pane. "You see," he said,
"Everything's as she left it when she died.
Her sons won't sell the house or the things in it.
They say they mean to come and summer here
Where they were boys. They haven't come this year.
They live so far away—one is out West—
It will be hard for them to keep their word.
Anyway they won't have the place disturbed."
A buttoned haircloth lounge spread scrolling arms
Under a crayon portrait on the wall,
Done sadly from an old daguerreotype.
"That was the father as he went to war.
She always, when she talked about the war,
Sooner or later came and leaned, half knelt,
Against the lounge beside it, though I doubt
If such unlifelike lines kept power to stir
Anything in her after all the years.
He fell at Gettysburg or Fredericksburg,
I ought to know—it makes a difference which:
Fredericksburg wasn't Gettysburg, of course.
But what I'm getting to is how forsaken

A little cottage this has always seemed;
Since she went, more than ever, but before—
I don't mean altogether by the lives
That had gone out of it, the father first,
Then the two sons, till she was left alone.
(Nothing could draw her after those two sons.
She valued the considerate neglect
She had at some cost taught them after years.)
I mean by the world's having passed it by—
As we almost got by this afternoon.
It always seems to me a sort of mark
To measure how far fifty years have brought us.
Why not sit down if you are in no haste?
These doorsteps seldom have a visitor.
The warping boards pull out their own old nails
With none to tread and put them in their place.
She had her own idea of things, the old lady.
And she liked talk. She had seen Garrison
And Whittier, and had her story of them.
One wasn't long in learning that she thought,
Whatever else the Civil War was for,
It wasn't just to keep the States together,
Nor just to free the slaves, though it did both.
She wouldn't have believed those ends enough
To have given outright for them all she gave.
Her giving somehow touched the principle
That all men are created free and equal.
And to hear her quaint phrases—so removed
From the world's view today of all those things.
That's a hard mystery of Jefferson's.
What did he mean? Of course the easy way
Is to decide it simply isn't true.
It may not be. I heard a fellow say so.
But never mind, the Welshman got it planted
Where it will trouble us a thousand years.
Each age will have to reconsider it.
You couldn't tell her what the West was saying,
And what the South, to her serene belief.
She had some art of hearing and yet not
Hearing the latter wisdom of the world.
White was the only race she ever knew.
Black she had scarcely seen, and yellow never.
But how could they be made so very unlike
By the same hand working in the same stuff?

She had supposed the war decided that.
What are you going to do with such a person?
Strange how such innocence gets its own way.
I shouldn't be surprised if in this world
It were the force that would at last prevail.
Do you know but for her there was a time
When, to please younger members of the church,
Or rather say non-members in the church,
Whom we all have to think of nowadays,
I would have changed the Creed a very little?
Not that she ever had to ask me not to;
It never got so far as that; but the bare thought
Of her old tremulous bonnet in the pew,
And of her half asleep, was too much for me.
Why, I might wake her up and startle her.
It was the words 'descended into Hades'
That seemed too pagan to our liberal youth.
You know they suffered from a general onslaught.
And well, if they weren't true why keep right on
Saying them like the heathen? We could drop them.
Only—there was the bonnet in the pew.
Such a phrase couldn't have meant much to her.
But suppose she had missed it from the Creed,
As a child misses the unsaid Good-night
And falls asleep with heartache—how should *I* feel?
I'm just as glad she made me keep hands off,
For, dear me, why abandon a belief
Merely because it ceases to be true.
Cling to it long enough, and not a doubt
It will turn true again, for so it goes.
Most of the change we think we see in life
Is due to truths being in and out of favor.
As I sit here, and oftentimes, I wish
I could be monarch of a desert land
I could devote and dedicate forever
To the truths we keep coming back and back to.
So desert it would have to be, so walled
By mountain ranges half in summer snow,
No one would covet it or think it worth
The pains of conquering to force change on.
Scattered oases where men dwelt, but mostly
Sand dunes held loosely in tamarisk
Blown over and over themselves in idleness.
Sand grains should sugar in the natal dew

The babe born to the desert, the sandstorm
Retard mid-waste my cowering caravans—

"There are bees in this wall." He struck the clapboards,
Fierce heads looked out; small bodies pivoted.
We rose to go. Sunset blazed on the windows.

"Home is the place where, when you have to go there,
They have to take you in."

"I should have called it
Something you somehow haven't to deserve."

3. *Lawrence*

Robert Frost's father died in California in 1885. The boy, together with his mother and younger sister, accompanied the coffined body back across the continent. Home was now a textile city called Lawrence, in Massachusetts.

Never would Robert Frost lose the sights and sounds of San Francisco. They remained brilliant and frightening decades later: the street gangs, the toughs, his father's torchlit political rallies, the guns, mobs, and strangers. And behind all this, the great Pacific—the brute voice of the Pacific shaking the misty strand, promising something dire for the land.

As the train moved east across empty deserts and mountains to the Mississippi Valley (which had put New England farming out of business) it seemed to be rolling up the whole brief scroll of Will Frost's extravagant life. Death gave no judgment or release to the eleven-year-old boy; it hushed all questions and confirmed in him his own fire and ice.

His father had fancied himself a rebel. William Prescott Frost, Jr., allowed no one to forget that as a high-school boy he had run away from Lawrence and tried to join General Lee's Army of Virginia. Later this handsome, swaggering young man had performed brilliantly at Harvard and cut a swath through the tavern society of Cambridge. After graduating, he scorned New England, all he knew of it: his stiff moralizing father, his prim scolding mother, the grimy brick-walled life of a mill town. West! As far the land would allow, marrying Belle Moodie on the way and becoming a newspaperman in San Francisco. In that brawling city, swept by silver sandals and run by railroad Republicans, he became an active Democrat, called himself a Copperhead, and named his firstborn Robert Lee.

Will Frost succeeded as a newsman and editor. He loved politics, sported in its intrigue and pageantry. He earned little money but made many noisy friends. Among them he could forget the weakness in his lungs and his recurrent terrible depressions. But he neglected himself and

31

his family, tried to stave off consumption through athletic contests or drink. At thirty-four he was dead.

For Robert Frost, his father would always be a compelling force: moodily harsh or indulgent, always demanding and unpredictable—an Old Testament Jahweh whom he would fear and worship and in many petty ways emulate.

Robert's mother was a different kind, a Scottish transplant raised in Ohio. His parents had met and married in Pennsylvania where they were, for one year, all there was of staff in a small private school.

. . . my paternal ancestor came here some time in the sixteen hundreds . . . , but . . . my mother was an immigrant. She came to these shores from Edinburgh in an old vessel that docked at Philadelphia. But she felt the spirit of America and became a part of it even before she set her foot off the boat.

She used to tell us about it when I was a child. She was sitting on the deck of the boat waiting for orders to come ashore. Near her some workmen were loading Delaware peaches. . . . One of them picked out one and dropped it into her lap.

"Here, take that," he said. The way he said it and the spirit in which he gave it left an indelible impression on her mind. . . .

Looking back would I say that she was less the American than my father? No. . . . He took it for granted. He was a Fourth-of-July American. . . . She . . . was a year-round American.

Graceful and intense, brown-eyed Isabelle Moodie was a born teacher. She fought no currents, she was sustained by them. However disorderly her classrooms might have seemed, she flowed with the excitement of young minds. Reading aloud to her pupils, she inspired them with stories of William Wallace and Robert Bruce, great heroes, doers of splendid deeds. Moreover, voices spoke to her and she believed them. She believed in a kindly God. When she died of cancer, fifteen years after settling in New England, she was still sustained, certain of the peace she was going to.

All his life these two would contend in Robert Frost: the teacher and the political schemer; the believer in heroes, the manipulator of crowds. Never would he outlive them or escape their company. The gentleness of the trusting heart was bred in him, but no less the blood-fever of a man of action. Whatever the boy would become as a thinker and writer would be struck from the tensions of opposites.

Back then to the cold Atlantic shore, to the beginning of beginnings, where six generations of Frosts had scratched a living in the glacial till. Back from San Francisco to Grandfather Frost's place in Lawrence, where sober work governed the six days and God still ruled a-Sunday.

It was predestined, of course—so Frost came to believe—this returning to the source, but that would take him another thirty years to discover, in Derry, New Hampshire, and in old England across the sea.

Once by the Pacific

The shattered water made a misty din.
Great waves looked over others coming in,
And thought of doing something to the shore
That water never did to land before.
The clouds were low and hairy in the skies,
Like locks blown forward in the gleam of eyes.
You could not tell, and yet it looked as if
The shore was lucky in being backed by cliff,
The cliff in being backed by continent;
It looked as if a night of dark intent
Was coming, and not only a night, an age.
Someone had better be prepared for rage.
There would be more than ocean-water broken
Before God's last *Put out the Light* was spoken.

The Onset

Always the same, when on a fated night
At last the gathered snow lets down as white
As may be in dark woods, and with a song
It shall not make again all winter long
Of hissing on the yet uncovered ground,
I almost stumble looking up and around,
As one who overtaken by the end
Gives up his errand, and lets death descend
Upon him where he is, with nothing done
To evil, no important triumph won,
More than if life had never been begun.

Yet all the precedent is on my side:
I know that winter death has never tried
The earth but it has failed: the snow may heap
In long storms an undrifted four feet deep
As measured against maple, birch, and oak,
It cannot check the peeper's silver croak;
And I shall see the snow all go downhill
In water of a slender April rill
That flashes tail through last year's withered brake
And dead weeds, like a disappearing snake.
Nothing will be left white but here a birch,
And there a clump of houses with a church.

The Telephone

"When I was just as far as I could walk
From here today,
There was an hour
All still
When leaning with my head against a flower
I heard you talk.
Don't say I didn't, for I heard you say—
You spoke from that flower on the windowsill—
Do you remember what it was you said?"

"First tell me what it was you thought you heard."

"Having found the flower and driven a bee away,
I leaned my head,
And holding by the stalk,
I listened and I thought I caught the word—
What was it? Did you call me by my name?
Or did you say—
Someone said 'Come'—I heard it as I bowed."

"I may have thought as much, but not aloud."

"Well, so I came."

The Tuft of Flowers

I went to turn the grass once after one
Who mowed it in the dew before the sun.

The dew was gone that made his blade so keen
Before I came to view the leveled scene.

I looked for him behind an isle of trees;
I listened for his whetstone on the breeze.

But he had gone his way, the grass all mown,
And I must be, as he had been—alone,

"As all must be," I said within my heart,
"Whether they work together or apart."

But as I said it, swift there passed me by
On noiseless wing a bewildered butterfly,

Seeking with memories grown dim o'er night
Some resting flower of yesterday's delight.

And once I marked his flight go round and round,
As where some flower lay withering on the ground.

And then he flew as far as eye could see,
And then on tremulous wing came back to me.

I thought of questions that have no reply,
And would have turned to toss the grass to dry;

But he turned first, and led my eye to look
At a tall tuft of flowers beside a brook,

A leaping tongue of bloom the scythe had spared
Beside a reedy brook the scythe had bared.

The mower in the dew had loved them thus,
By leaving them to flourish, not for us,

Nor yet to draw one thought of ours to him,
But from sheer morning gladness at the brim.

The butterfly and I had lit upon,
Nevertheless, a message from the dawn,

That made me hear the wakening birds around,
And hear his long scythe whispering to the ground,

And feel a spirit kindred to my own;
So that henceforth I worked no more alone;

But glad with him, I worked as with his aid,
And weary, sought at noon with him the shade;

And dreaming, as it were, held brotherly speech
With one whose thought I had not hoped to reach.

"Men work together," I told him from the heart,
"Whether they work together or apart."

Nothing not built with hands of course is sacred.

4. Derry

"You were always deep in your thinking, Robert," his Aunt Blanche told him, "but slow to get it." Frost was twenty-six when, in the fall of 1900, he came to Derry to take up farming. It was a small farm on a piny hill in glacial pothole country. Frost drove up in a wagon, with a silent wife and one child where there should have been two.

After years of jobs tried and jobs quit, shoemaking, newspapering, mill jobs, teaching in his mother's schools, college, chickens—after years of rejected poems, buried poems, he found himself the indentured tenant on a rundown farm near a small New Hampshire village. Farming in Derry was not his choice, it was exile. He was a poet, not a farmer. But his doctor, owing to Frost's repeated lung infections and to the weakness for tuberculosis in the family, had insisted that he get out of the city, take up life in the country. And his wife, Elinor, and all his relatives, had agreed with the decision. Frost acquiesced, unable to think of any other way.

In truth, after all those years, what had he to look back upon for strength? A wife (co-valedictorian at Lawrence High), and one poem published six years before ($15).

And what had he to go forward with? Only obstinacy. Only the brute guts to go ahead, make poems.

For Elinor Frost the sudden shift from teaching in Belle Frost's little school to dirt farming in Derry was no less an act of desperation. In high school her life and Robert's had been all promise: he would go to Dartmouth College, she to St. Lawrence University. But after a few months Robert had quit Dartmouth and demanded that she leave St. Lawrence to devote herself to him. That she liked the university and wanted to go on, he couldn't understand. Nor would he listen. Their meetings turned to battles; truces led only to new demands and fits of jealousy. Twice Robert had stormed off, once all the way to Carolina, threatening suicide. Over three years his courtship became nothing less than a siege. And at last she had yielded. Still there was no end of trouble. Robert's teaching wore him out, put him in a rage about his poetry. After Elliott was born, Robert had sallied off to Harvard to study Latin—there was hope in that—but then, after three semesters, when Lesley was born, he had quit his studies again.

At the beginning of summer Elliott took sick with *cholera infantum*. So quick it happened: two days sick, one night worse, next day dead. Nothing to do, the doctor had said, angry at not being called in time.

After that, listless with despair, Elinor played her part in finding the farm, but she couldn't hope that farming was the way for them. Something would come up to bring on a new convulsion and overthrow what little plan they seemed to have.

Grandfather Frost had financed the purchase of the farm. Last of the farmers in the family, he had early observed the decline in agriculture throughout New England and had sold out to take a job in the textile mills in Lawrence. A certain stern piousness and careful attention to small details had eventually earned him the position of foreman in a cotton print factory. He couldn't hope that farming would revive in Derry, but something had to be done to bring Robert back to earth. Rob talked of writing poetry, but talk was all it amounted to. Talk, talk, the whole night long, then sleep all morning. Intelligent talk too, sometimes; full of unusual knowledge. Rob was like his father, a clever fellow gone wrong—headstrong, undisciplined, neglectful of responsibilities. There wasn't a grateful bone in his body, nor a moderate one. Robert was just plain lazy, and given to fits of temper—tantrums, that is what they were. A judge in town had fined him $10 for starting a brawl in a neighbor's apartment, publicly called him "riffraff." No Frost had ever been called riffraff before.

It's a distressing thing to have a poet in the family. That's the one conviction that all nations share.

And kinfolk can't abide. So Grandfather Frost, seventy-seven years old, bought the Derry farm in a last effort to succor his only male heir: $1,700; another $25 for the fresh-cut hay in the barn. Then he arranged for Rob's best friend, Carl Burell, to come and help with the work.

Grandfather Frost was more generous and more canny than Robert ever admitted. In addition to buying the farm he gave Rob a $500 annuity. In Derry in 1900 that was a sizable cash crop which few farms could count on. It paid taxes, provided furniture, and allowed the family to take summer vacations in northern New Hampshire and Vermont, away from the annual miseries of hay fever.

In his will Grandfather Frost wrote one stipulation: Robert was to have the farm without rent, but it would not become *his* farm until he had lived there ten years. How he would manage for ten years was something Robert would have to work out for himself.

Little there was to encourage either the poet or the farmer in Derry. Although Derry had already passed through its leanest years and was, thanks to the railroad from Boston, already reviving, farming would share little in the growing prosperity. The Middle Atlantic states and the Midwest were crowding the East with eggs and milk, the market in ice was gone, wool all done, timber cut over. Derry people had turned to manufacturing. Two shoe factories were running, and a knit shop, and some specialty wood plants turning out windows and sashes— these provided most of the work. There was talk of a daily paper and of constructing an electric-car line to Manchester. But apart from having a fine high school—Pinkerton Academy—given to the town by two merchants of the Revolutionary period, there was little to distinguish Derry from a score of other towns in upper New England. Big prosperous milk factories, like the H. P. Hood place, might still provide a good life, but except for them farming would never be more than a poor man's subsistence.

Furthermore, Robert Frost knew precious little about farming. As a youngster he had been sent off summers to work on farms in Salem and Windham, where he had received an education in haying. And more recently he'd taken a graduate course in eggs given by a flock of white Wyandottes. That was the size of his farming background.

And yet . . . here was "the Magoon place": thirty acres of fields, orchard, and woodlot; a well, a garden plot, a rock garden for flowers; a white clapboard house and ell with shed and barn attached, a bay window to the front, a sunny piazza to the south . . .

Down the road from the farm, on the way into town, was West-Running Brook. The first colonists had settled here when they came up from the coast, long before the Revolution. John Stark had been raised here. The name itself—West-Running Brook—took Robert's fancy: in a land where all streams flow steadfastly east and south, here was a contrary one taking its time meandering west.

Soft October light—summer's last benediction—the trees all gone to color, and away in the north the twin humps of the Uncanoonucs standing blue above the bronzing horizon. No steely breath had yet laid the flowers low. The boughs of the old apple trees hung down to the grass with their ruby treasure. When Carl Burell arrived, bringing his eighty-four-year-old grandfather, Jonathan Eastman, the two at once set to work picking apples, boxing up the best and shipping them off to market. After that there were chicken coops to knock together for Robert's three hundred Wyandottes, a cow and a horse to buy with money provided by Grandfather Frost, firewood to get in, and boughs to bank the house against the onset of the first wet flakes of winter.

Carl Burell was not a farmer, but, born in Vermont, the lore was in his bones. He'd migrated to New Hampshire, working at a variety of jobs both before and after high school, and had become a jack-of-all-trades. Carl and old Jont Eastman seemed to know, with not much more than a glance around, what needed to be done to get the farm back in working order. Calmly they went about it, not pressing time, not wasting it, and making light of the long days with exchanges of banter. For a year and a half Carl and Jont lived on the farm. While there wasn't much to be made of so small a place, they did what they could. And Frost learned the work. He cared little for it, especially having to get up at cock's crow, but nevertheless he began to listen with a farmer's ear and sniff the weather with a farmer's nose.

After November drizzles, the snow set in. This was a hard time for Elinor. The home wasn't straightened round yet. An artist herself, she hated the bother of housekeeping. Water spilled on the kitchen floor as like as not was left to turn to ice, and mud and slop walked in on every pair of boots. Snow isolated the farm; it seemed to push back all other people beyond reach. For long spells Elinor would stand at a window looking out, seeming not to see the white powder whirling down from the eaves. Little Elliott's grave back in Lawrence lay between the mounds of Will and Belle. Sudden and swift life gave way, and then all sign of it was smoothed over. She could not forget, but what she saw was only blankness too featureless to express.

Nor was winter easier for Robert to bear. Elliott's grave seemed but the heap of his own failures. He had been too preoccupied with himself to take notice of the boy's sickness. It was

God's judgment, surely it was God's just wrath visited upon him for his selfishness and neglect. Elinor scorned such self-pity. It was senseless to see something personal in what had happened. Elliott's dying was a meaningless act of nature—all life was meaningless. Thus the death of their first child stood between Elinor and Robert like a pane of morning ice, distorting what they saw in each other and crazing the reflections of themselves.

Five years of marriage had turned this serious girl into a silent woman. For a while at the university she had hoped to make a life for herself, in poetry and painting perhaps, but Robert had come on her like a despot. Robert was a force beyond her strength to control, and beyond his. There was madness in him, as there was in his sister Jeanie, and had been in his father. There was also (what few people knew) a childlike nature in him, fearful of the dark, defenseless, yet eager and curious and full of wonderment as well.

In any case it was settled: for better or worse she was married to Robert Frost. Something more than her love and her need was wed to this difficult man. He would always expect her to admire him, delight in his poems, give herself unquestioningly to be his servant, mother, wife. And she would have to play those roles to the end. If there was a poet in Robert Frost—as she believed—it might take the dissolution of herself to nurture him. Sometimes it seemed that way.

Storm Fear

When the wind works against us in the dark,
And pelts with snow
The lower-chamber window on the east,
And whispers with a sort of stifled bark,
The beast,
"Come out! Come out!"—
It costs no inward struggle not to go,
Ah, no!
I count our strength,
Two and a child,
Those of us not asleep subdued to mark
How the cold creeps as the fire dies at length—
How drifts are piled,
Dooryard and road ungraded,
Till even the comforting barn grows far away,
And my heart owns a doubt
Whether 'tis in us to arise with day
And save ourselves unaided.

Home Burial

He saw her from the bottom of the stairs
Before she saw him. She was starting down,
Looking back over her shoulder at some fear.
She took a doubtful step and then undid it
To raise herself and look again. He spoke
Advancing toward her: "What is it you see
From up there always?—for I want to know."
She turned and sank upon her skirts at that,
And her face changed from terrified to dull.
He said to gain time: "What is it you see?"
Mounting until she cowered under him.
"I will find out now—you must tell me, dear."
She, in her place, refused him any help,
With the least stiffening of her neck and silence.
She let him look, sure that he wouldn't see,
Blind creature; and awhile he didn't see.
But at last he murmured, "Oh," and again, "Oh."

"What is it—what?" she said.

                              "Just that I see."

"You don't," she challenged. "Tell me what it is."

"The wonder is I didn't see at once.
I never noticed it from here before.
I must be wonted to it—that's the reason.
The little graveyard where my people are!
So small the window frames the whole of it.
Not so much larger than a bedroom, is it?
There are three stones of slate and one of marble,
Broad-shouldered little slabs there in the sunlight
On the sidehill. We haven't to mind *those*.
But I understand: it is not the stones,
But the child's mound——"

       "Don't, don't, don't,
 don't," she cried.

She withdrew, shrinking from beneath his arm
That rested on the banister, and slid downstairs;
And turned on him with such a daunting look,
He said twice over before he knew himself:
"Can't a man speak of his own child he's lost?"

"Not you—Oh, where's my hat? Oh, I don't need it!
I must get out of here. I must get air.—
I don't know rightly whether any man can."

"Amy! Don't go to someone else this time.
Listen to me. I won't come down the stairs."
He sat and fixed his chin between his fists.
"There's something I should like to ask you, dear."

"You don't know how to ask it."
        "Help me, then."

Her fingers moved the latch for all reply.

"My words are nearly always an offense.
I don't know how to speak of anything
So as to please you. But I might be taught,
I should suppose. I can't say I see how.
A man must partly give up being a man
With womenfolk. We could have some arrangement
By which I'd bind myself to keep hands off
Anything special you're a-mind to name.
Though I don't like such things 'twixt those that love.
Two that don't love can't live together without them.
But two that do can't live together with them."
She moved the latch a little. "Don't—don't go.
Don't carry it to someone else this time.
Tell me about it if it's something human.
Let me into your grief. I'm not so much
Unlike other folks as your standing there
Apart would make me out. Give me my chance.
I do think, though, you overdo it a little.
What was it brought you up to think it the thing
To take your mother-loss of a first child
So inconsolably—in the face of love.
You'd think his memory might be satisfied——"

"There you go sneering now!"

         "I'm not, I'm not!
You make me angry. I'll come down to you.
God, what a woman! And it's come to this,
A man can't speak of his own child that's dead."

"You can't because you don't know how to speak.
If you had any feelings, you that dug
With your own hand—how could you?—his little grave;
I saw you from that very window there,
Making the gravel leap and leap in air,
Leap up, like that, like that, and land so lightly
And roll back down the mound beside the hole.
I thought, Who is that man? I didn't know you.
And I crept down the stairs and up the stairs
To look again, and still your spade kept lifting.
Then you came in. I heard your rumbling voice
Out in the kitchen, and I don't know why,
But I went near to see with my own eyes.
You could sit there with the stains on your shoes
Of the fresh earth from your own baby's grave
And talk about your everyday concerns.
You had stood the spade up against the wall
Outside there in the entry, for I saw it."

"I shall laugh the worst laugh I ever laughed.
I'm cursed. God, if I don't believe I'm cursed."

"I can repeat the very words you were saying:
'Three foggy mornings and one rainy day
Will rot the best birch fence a man can build.'
Think of it, talk like that at such a time!
What had how long it takes a birch to rot
To do with what was in the darkened parlor?
You *couldn't* care! The nearest friends can go
With anyone to death, comes so far short
They might as well not try to go at all.
No, from the time when one is sick to death,
One is alone, and he dies more alone.
Friends make pretense of following to the grave,
But before one is in it, their minds are turned
And making the best of their way back to life
And living people, and things they understand.
But the world's evil. I won't have grief so
If I can change it. Oh, I won't, I won't!"

45

"There, you have said it all and you feel better.
You won't go now. You're crying. Close the door.
The heart's gone out of it: why keep it up?
Amy! There's someone coming down the road!"

"*You*—oh, you think the talk is all. I must go—
Somewhere out of this house. How can I make you——"

"If—you—do!" She was opening the door wider.
"Where do you mean to go? First tell me that.
I'll follow and bring you back by force. I *will*!—"

. . . If the day ever comes when they know who
They are, they may know better where they are.

5. Apprenticeship in New England

Wasn't there something special in the sounds of voices? Something beyond words, alive, like the fibers of an elm running intertwined from one end of the message to the other?

. . . "Sakes,
It's only weather." . . .

I s'pose I've got to go the road I'm going:
Other folks have to, and why shouldn't I?

"When was I ever anything but kind to him?
But I'll not have the fellow back." . . .

The sense was in the sounds of the voices more than in words, mere fragments of meaning. The technical things people liked to talk about—iamb, anapest, elision, or irony, sarcasm, pathos —were only labels for what the voice instinctively knew. The voice showed how a person carried himself into trouble, or through trouble; it was like a gesture of anger or defiance or hopelessness, whatever. Was it not character speaking? In the voice itself and in the situation?

"I'm cursed! God, if I don't believe I'm cursed."

". . . His brother's rich,
A somebody—director in the bank."

Just the pure sounds. As the first half-humans must have uttered them before there were words. That showed the grain of a man or woman bending with or resisting some special strain.

A friend, thinking to be helpful, told Frost that his poems sounded "too much like talk," and prescribed a study of Sidney Lanier. The advice was rejected of course, but the chance remark came as a revelation: the natural sounds of talk were what he had been reaching for in his writing. Something as sure of itself as that. The human voice needed no instruction: it caught the tones exactly, even as the emotion was stumbling into words.

Frost had first recognized those voice-sounds while sneaking time away from work in a mill, hiding out and reading Palgrave's *Golden Treasury*. Shakespeare, he discovered, had caught the tones, especially when there was action going on. Wordsworth had caught them in his early poems. But those voices were in books; one had to listen for them with the imagination. Now he could hear authentic voices all around him: in gossip, in the way people told stories in town, in the intonations of his French-Canadian neighbor; and most of all, day by day, he heard them from Carl Burell and old Jont Eastman warming up after chores, sitting with their elbows propped on the kitchen table. They were just talking in that pictured drawl of rural people, recounting the antics of animals and children or the rueful carryings-on of adults.

That winter Frost began again to write. Late at night when all the household was asleep, sitting in a comfortable chair with a board across the arms, once more he followed words out to see where they would lead. At first he copied over all his old poems, testing whether other words or rhymes would carry his meanings further. Then he began to try new voices in new situations, to hear what they would discover for themselves. That was the way writing worked best for him.

Night shut him in, forced him to find or make his own society. Whatever it was that started him off—some snatch of conversation, some impulse or wish or vision—it had to have time to work its way into words:

> . . . a fresh access
> Of wind that caught against the house a moment,
> Gulped snow, and then blew free again . . .
>
> "You can just see it glancing off the roof
> Making a great scroll upward toward the sky,
> Long enough for recording all our names on.—"

Writing late at night, to the steamy sounds in the kitchen stove and the peaceful snoring of old Jont upstairs, he would often sleep through the morning chores. The Jersey cow, stamping and bawling in the barn, would protest having to live by such a schedule; then Carl would calmly go hay her and milk her, separate the cream, and sell what the family didn't need. The cow and chickens were supposed to be Robert's part of the farm work, but Carl was not a calculator. He too wrote poetry that didn't sell. Besides, the Jersey was a good cow; no profit in letting her go dry.

In the spring Elinor, too, began to revive. Sometime between crow shouts in February and crocus shoots in April, Elinor's heart thawed. The glitter of icicles lightening to water along the southern eaves turned her from her arctic introspection to talk of the garden, and of the flowers she would set out in the rocky bank between two sugar maples.

Hot spells in May and June transformed the farm. Lesley, toddling barefoot outside, conveyed to the rest of the family her excitement over this new world. Even the practical Carl, knowing they should be plowing and planting, could not resist the springing things. Out back, beyond the orchard and hay field, at the source of the little stream Frost called Hyla Brook, was an alder swamp where ferns were uncoiling and the first orchids coming to life again. Let the farm go for a while; it wouldn't stray far.

Long ago when he and Robert were in school together, Carl had taken his young friend "botanizing," shown him where to look for the most secret and delicate species, shown him his volumes of pressed flowers, all carefully labeled according to Linnaeus's system. He had lent Robert his books, the works of Darwin and Huxley, and Proctor's volume on stars, *Our Place Among Infinities*. These had opened the world of natural science to the city boy, a world feared by his spiritual mother and overlooked by his rough and ready father. Creation or Evolution— he and Carl had endlessly debated that question without settling it.

One could argue about what men said in books, but here were the live flowers springing up, in all their form and color; always the identical patterns in the same shady places, spring after spring, century after century—an elegant performance endlessly repeated. For Carl, spring flowers no less than the parade of planets among the fixed stars were an assurance of meaning beyond mystery: some unchanging force of Nature *must* be fulfilling its plan throughout the heavens as on earth. There must be a design, even though he could not know what it was.

In such an argument Frost could follow Carl only partway. Nature was continuity and fidelity to form, beyond a doubt, but it was blankness and terror too. Between the stars there was nothing, absolute nothing at absolute zero. What purpose could be seen in that? Or in the oceans—cell, jellyfish, vertebrate, man. Only man claimed to find a meaning in such accidents of survival. Down the road across West-Running Brook lived a woman widowed thirty-seven years since her husband went off to the Civil War; what frail human hope carried her across such a waste of solitude? Or the crusty miller who jammed an old Indian into the paddles in his millrace to settle once and for all an ancient blood-grudge. Frost knew both men in himself: the astonished Indian and the enraged white man. Hate, vengeance, cruelty—Nature made too much of them. At night at the farm, Nature was the thousand eyes that kept watch on him, the things outside the house that barked and howled and groaned at him. Where was any cosmic plan in that? Surely the dead were holding something back.

Spring planting—summer haying—autumn harvesting—fall colors—first frost—apples again; then wood to split, snow falling, and time to think about all the things to do when spring came round again. Perhaps it was the peace of the old farm, or just the never-ending small jobs which mark the passage through one season into the next. However it came about, something of hope and strength returned to Elinor and Robert Frost which finally reconciled them to Nature's ways. After August, Elinor was carrying a new baby.

Old Jont died during the second winter and Carl, sensing that he wasn't needed anymore, moved out to take another job. It was time for Robert to take charge of his farm. He would have to learn to manage the horse, and he would have to learn to milk and strip the cow; that would be hard on the cow but good for Robert.

Frost never spoke gratefully of Carl; that was not in his nature. But Carl departed peaceably enough. He understood his friend's needs. Carl was an original, one of those self-educated Yankees whose slow speech disguised a philosophic mind and resourceful character. He would never make much money, but neither did he think a lot of money. With his capable hands and his adventuring spirit he would find a place for himself on this planet. Perhaps it was in cryptic recognition of Carl that Frost, much later, said:

. . . one of the things that makes you go [as a poet] is making a hero out of somebody that nobody else had ever noticed was a hero.

The years immediately following those first two winters in Derry were among the happiest the Frosts ever knew. One by one new children came along, one by one drafts of new poems. Something began to solidify in Frost and take shape. His poems were not ready yet for a book, but the way words led on to words gave him confidence. And while Elinor would never resign herself to the loss of her firstborn, the shrill voices of the living broke in on the awful silences of the grave.

Lesley, Carol, Irma, Marjorie: running feet through the house, yelling voices in the yard. The poet heard their excitement and his better nature—that of a child—began to run with them.

That other Frost, the dark primitive who lurked in a cave of terrors, would never be entirely civilized; he too is part of every man's nature. One night when she was eleven, Lesley was dragged from bed by her father, who, brandishing a pistol, demanded that she choose between him and her weeping mother: one, he promised, would be dead by morning. The cause of this sudden storm is unknown, and fortunately the squall blew itself out without the choice having to be made. There lived in Frost the shouting bully, twin brother to the abject penitent, and many another melodramatic, witty, clowning, generous, ruthless character as well. Only very slowly, only much later, with success and public acclaim, would they become a somewhat settled society within him.

By 1906, when a few poems began to sell, Frost gave up farming. With the help of friends, and his excellent record at Harvard, he found a job at Pinkerton Academy where he was soon recognized to be an exceptional teacher. After four years at Pinkerton he was invited to teach literature, philosophy, and psychology at the Normal School in Plymouth, New Hampshire.

Derry was destiny for him, and time was its essential element. Time was the one thing this restless young man had never allowed himself. Old Grandfather Frost, now dead, had understood his grandson better than he imagined. Ten years, his grandfather had demanded. Ten years it had to be, forty seasons.

Out of that frustrated but determined man began to come a "sheaf of poems" which would slowly grow into eleven books. Sensual memories, patterns of color and speech, the dramas of plain people, their suffering, humor, meanness, and moments of heroism—all began to find their forms and fit themselves with words. Some of his visions would be twenty or thirty years clarifying—poems too need time—but with few exceptions his poetry welled up in the springs of Derry and were uncovered by a man who had blundered through a quarrel with himself and become an original voice, a poet.

To the Thawing Wind

Come with rain, O loud Southwester!
Bring the singer, bring the nester;
Give the buried flower a dream;
Make the settled snowbank steam;
Find the brown beneath the white;
But whate'er you do tonight,
Bathe my window, make it flow,
Melt it as the ice will go;
Melt the glass and leave the sticks
Like a hermit's crucifix;
Burst into my narrow stall;
Swing the picture on the wall;
Run the rattling pages o'er;
Scatter poems on the floor;
Turn the poet out of door.

Two Tramps in Mud Time

Out of the mud two strangers came
And caught me splitting wood in the yard.
And one of them put me off my aim
By hailing cheerily "Hit them hard!"
I knew pretty well why he dropped behind
And let the other go on a way.
I knew pretty well what he had in mind:
He wanted to take my job for pay.

Good blocks of oak it was I split,
As large around as the chopping block;
And every piece I squarely hit
Fell splinterless as a cloven rock.
The blows that a life of self-control
Spares to strike for the common good,
That day, giving a loose to my soul,
I spent on the unimportant wood.

The sun was warm but the wind was chill.
You know how it is with an April day
When the sun is out and the wind is still,
You're one month on in the middle of May.
But if you so much as dare to speak,
A cloud comes over the sunlit arch,
A wind comes off a frozen peak,
And you're two months back in the middle of March.

A bluebird comes tenderly up to alight
And turns to the wind to unruffle a plume,
His song so pitched as not to excite
A single flower as yet to bloom.
It is snowing a flake: and he half knew
Winter was only playing possum.
Except in color he isn't blue,
But he wouldn't advise a thing to blossom.

The water for which we may have to look
In summertime with a witching wand,
In every wheelrut's now a brook,
In every print of a hoof a pond.
Be glad of water, but don't forget
The lurking frost in the earth beneath
That will steal forth after the sun is set
And show on the water its crystal teeth.

The time when most I loved my task
These two must make me love it more
By coming with what they came to ask.
You'd think I never had felt before
The weight of an ax-head poised aloft,
The grip on earth of outspread feet,
The life of muscles rocking soft
And smooth and moist in vernal heat.

Out of the woods two hulking tramps
(From sleeping God knows where last night,
But not long since in the lumber camps).
They thought all chopping was theirs of right.
Men of the woods and lumberjacks,
They judged me by their appropriate tool.
Except as a fellow handled an ax
They had no way of knowing a fool.

Nothing on either side was said.
They knew they had but to stay their stay
And all their logic would fill my head:
As that I had no right to play
With what was another man's work for gain.
My right might be love but theirs was need.
And where the two exist in twain
Theirs was the better right—agreed.

But yield who will to their separation,
My object in living is to unite
My avocation and my vocation
As my two eyes make one in sight.
Only where love and need are one,
And the work is play for mortal stakes,
Is the deed ever really done
For Heaven and the future's sakes.

Hyla Brook

By June our brook's run out of song and speed.
Sought for much after that, it will be found
Either to have gone groping underground
(And taken with it all the Hyla breed
That shouted in the mist a month ago,
Like ghost of sleigh bells in a ghost of snow)—
Or flourished and come up in jewelweed,
Weak foliage that is blown upon and bent,
Even against the way its waters went.
Its bed is left a faded paper sheet
Of dead leaves stuck together by the heat—
A brook to none but who remember long.
This as it will be seen is other far
Than with brooks taken otherwhere in song.
We love the things we love for what they are.

After Apple-Picking

My long two-pointed ladder's sticking through a tree
Toward heaven still,
And there's a barrel that I didn't fill
Beside it, and there may be two or three
Apples I didn't pick upon some bough.
But I am done with apple-picking now.
Essence of winter sleep is on the night,
The scent of apples: I am drowsing off.
I cannot rub the strangeness from my sight
I got from looking through a pane of glass
I skimmed this morning from the drinking trough
And held against the world of hoary grass.
It melted, and I let it fall and break.
But I was well
Upon my way to sleep before it fell,
And I could tell
What form my dreaming was about to take.
Magnified apples appear and disappear,
Stem end and blossom end,
And every fleck of russet showing clear.
My instep arch not only keeps the ache,
It keeps the pressure of a ladder-round.
I feel the ladder sway as the boughs bend.
And I keep hearing from the cellar bin
The rumbling sound
Of load on load of apples coming in.
For I have had too much
Of apple-picking: I am overtired
Of the great harvest I myself desired.
There were ten thousand thousand fruit to touch,
Cherish in hand, lift down, and not let fall.
For all
That struck the earth,
No matter if not bruised or spiked with stubble,

Went surely to the cider-apple heap
As of no worth.
One can see what will trouble
This sleep of mine, whatever sleep it is.
Were he not gone,
The woodchuck could say whether it's like his
Long sleep, as I describe its coming on,
Or just some human sleep.

"Out, Out—"

The buzz saw snarled and rattled in the yard
And made dust and dropped stove-length sticks of wood,
Sweet-scented stuff when the breeze drew across it.
And from there those that lifted eyes could count
Five mountain ranges one behind the other
Under the sunset far into Vermont.
And the saw snarled and rattled, snarled and rattled,
As it ran light, or had to bear a load.
And nothing happened: day was all but done.
Call it a day, I wish they might have said
To please the boy by giving him the half hour
That a boy counts so much when saved from work.
His sister stood beside them in her apron
To tell them "Supper." At the word, the saw,
As if to prove saws knew what supper meant,
Leaped out at the boy's hand, or seemed to leap—
He must have given the hand. However it was,
Neither refused the meeting. But the hand!
The boy's first outcry was a rueful laugh,
As he swung toward them holding up the hand,
Half in appeal, but half as if to keep
The life from spilling. Then the boy saw all—
Since he was old enough to know, big boy
Doing a man's work, though a child at heart—
He saw all spoiled. "Don't let him cut my hand off—
The doctor, when he comes. Don't let him, sister!"
So. But the hand was gone already.
The doctor put him in the dark of ether.
He lay and puffed his lips out with his breath.
And then—the watcher at his pulse took fright.
No one believed. They listened at his heart.
Little—less—nothing!—and that ended it.
No more to build on there. And they, since they
Were not the one dead, turned to their affairs.

The Death of the Hired Man

Mary sat musing on the lamp-flame at the table,
Waiting for Warren. When she heard his step,
She ran on tiptoe down the darkened passage
To meet him in the doorway with the news
And put him on his guard. "Silas is back."
She pushed him outward with her through the door
And shut it after her. "Be kind," she said.
She took the market things from Warren's arms
And set them on the porch, then drew him down
To sit beside her on the wooden steps.

"When was I ever anything but kind to him?
But I'll not have the fellow back," he said.
"I told him so last haying, didn't I?
If he left then, I said, that ended it.
What good is he? Who else will harbor him
At his age for the little he can do?
What help he is there's no depending on.
Off he goes always when I need him most.
He thinks he ought to earn a little pay,
Enough at least to buy tobacco with,
So he won't have to beg and be beholden.
'All right,' I say, 'I can't afford to pay
Any fixed wages, though I wish I could.'
'Someone else can.' 'Then someone else will have to.'
I shouldn't mind his bettering himself
If that was what it was. You can be certain,
When he begins like that, there's someone at him
Trying to coax him off with pocket money—
In haying time, when any help is scarce.
In winter he comes back to us. I'm done."

"Sh! not so loud: he'll hear you," Mary said.

"I want him to: he'll have to soon or late."

"He's worn out. He's asleep beside the stove.
When I came up from Rowe's I found him here,
Huddled against the barn door fast asleep,
A miserable sight, and frightening, too—
You needn't smile—I didn't recognize him—
I wasn't looking for him—and he's changed.
Wait till you see."

         "Where did you say he'd been?"

"He didn't say. I dragged him to the house,
And gave him tea and tried to make him smoke.
I tried to make him talk about his travels.
Nothing would do: he just kept nodding off."

"What did he say? Did he say anything?"

"But little."

        "Anything? Mary, confess
He said he'd come to ditch the meadow for me."

"Warren!"

        "But did he? I just want to know."

"Of course he did. What would you have him say?
Surely you wouldn't grudge the poor old man
Some humble way to save his self-respect.
He added, if you really care to know,
He meant to clear the upper pasture, too.
That sounds like something you have heard before?
Warren, I wish you could have heard the way
He jumbled everything. I stopped to look
Two or three times—he made me feel so queer—
To see if he was talking in his sleep.
He ran on Harold Wilson—you remember—
The boy you had in haying four years since.
He's finished school, and teaching in his college.
Silas declares you'll have to get him back.
He says they two will make a team for work:
Between them they will lay this farm as smooth!
The way he mixed that in with other things.
He thinks young Wilson a likely lad, though daft
On education—you know how they fought
All through July under the blazing sun,
Silas up on the cart to build the load,
Harold along beside to pitch it on."

"Yes, I took care to keep well out of earshot."

"Well, those days trouble Silas like a dream.
You wouldn't think they would. How some things linger!
Harold's young college-boy's assurance piqued him.
After so many years he still keeps finding
Good arguments he sees he might have used.
I sympathize. I know just how it feels
To think of the right thing to say too late.
Harold's associated in his mind with Latin.
He asked me what I thought of Harold's saying
He studied Latin, like the violin,
Because he liked it—that an argument!
He said he couldn't make the boy believe
He could find water with a hazel prong—
Which showed how much good school had ever done him.
He wanted to go over that. But most of all
He thinks if he could have another chance
To teach him how to build a load of hay——"

"I know, that's Silas' one accomplishment.
He bundles every forkful in its place,
And tags and numbers it for future reference,
So he can find and easily dislodge it
In the unloading. Silas does that well.
He takes it out in bunches like big birds' nests.
You never see him standing on the hay
He's trying to lift, straining to lift himself."

"He thinks if he could teach him that, he'd be
Some good perhaps to someone in the world.
He hates to see a boy the fool of books.
Poor Silas, so concerned for other folk,
And nothing to look backward to with pride,
And nothing to look forward to with hope,
So now and never any different."

Part of a moon was falling down the west,
Dragging the whole sky with it to the hills.
Its light poured softly in her lap. She saw it
And spread her apron to it. She put out her hand
Among the harplike morning-glory strings,
Taut with the dew from garden bed to eaves,
As if she played unheard some tenderness
That wrought on him beside her in the night.

"Warren," she said, "he has come home to die:
You needn't be afraid he'll leave you this time."

"Home," he mocked gently.

                    "Yes, what else but home?
It all depends on what you mean by home.
Of course he's nothing to us, any more
Than was the hound that came a stranger to us
Out of the woods, worn out upon the trail."

"Home is the place where, when you have to go there,
They have to take you in."

                    "I should have called it
Something you somehow haven't to deserve."

Warren leaned out and took a step or two,
Picked up a little stick, and brought it back
And broke it in his hand and tossed it by.
"Silas has better claim on us you think
Than on his brother? Thirteen little miles
As the road winds would bring him to his door.
Silas has walked that far no doubt today.
Why doesn't he go there? His brother's rich,
A somebody—director in the bank."

"He never told us that."

                    "We know it, though."

"I think his brother ought to help, of course.
I'll see to that if there is need. He ought of right
To take him in, and might be willing to—
He may be better than appearances.
But have some pity on Silas. Do you think
If he had any pride in claiming kin
Or anything he looked for from his brother,
He'd keep so still about him all this time?"

"I wonder what's between them."

                    "I can tell you.
Silas is what he is—we wouldn't mind him—
But just the kind that kinsfolk can't abide.
He never did a thing so very bad.
He don't know why he isn't quite as good
As anybody. Worthless though he is,

He won't be made ashamed to please his brother."

"*I* can't think Si ever hurt anyone."

"No, but he hurt my heart the way he lay
And rolled his old head on that sharp-edged chair-back.
He wouldn't let me put him on the lounge.
You must go in and see what you can do.
I made the bed up for him there tonight.
You'll be surprised at him—how much he's broken.
His working days are done; I'm sure of it."

"I'd not be in a hurry to say that."

"I haven't been. Go, look, see for yourself.
But, Warren, please remember how it is:
He's come to help you ditch the meadow.
He has a plan. You mustn't laugh at him.
He may not speak of it, and then he may.
I'll sit and see if that small sailing cloud
Will hit or miss the moon."

              It hit the moon.
Then there were three there, making a dim row,
The moon, the little silver cloud, and she.

Warren returned—too soon, it seemed to her—
Slipped to her side, caught up her hand and waited.

"Warren?" she questioned.

              "Dead," was all he answered.

One luminary clock against the sky
Proclaimed the time was neither wrong nor right.

6. Old England

In the summer of 1912, having finished his servitude in Derry, Robert Frost packed up his family and moved to England. The sale of the farm, and the annuity from his grandfather, made the adventure possible. Frost had considered going to Vancouver where a friend and former student had settled, but instinct turned him to England. England was a land of writers, a commonwealth of poets.

For the first year the Frosts rented a cottage in Beaconsfield. (The blind Milton had lived hereabouts, and Grey, who woke such a stir of life in a country graveyard.) London was nearby, and though many changes had shocked its imperial power, it was still the center of the English-speaking world. In London Frost could sniff the shifting wind: the worldly illusions of *Pax Britannica* had lately been blown to shreds by stubborn Dutch farmers in South Africa; now new storms were making up in the Sudan, the Balkans, and in Russia and Germany. The old Queen was dead. With her, many a living poet had gone into obscurity. Brash new English voices were claiming the right to be heard. The Georgian Poets, a reaction to the Victorians, had already inspired other reactions, new experiments in writing, Free Verse and Imagism. Whatever all this newness might come to, Frost was glad to be in England. European weather was ominous but full of vitality.

Yet, for a while, Frost's business was with himself. Free at last from entanglements—cows, kinfolk, students, chickens—he had to face himself and his aging sheaf of poems. In twenty years he had sold but a handful of poems. Drafts he had, more than enough for one book, but it was time to be done with drafting. Even Elinor, his best and sharpest critic, could not help him now. No one could help him. His "influences"—a motley group of loners and explorers such as Leif Eriksen, Turgenev, Shakespeare, William James, Lucretius, Thoreau—withdrew into the shadows of his mind. He was alone, ready or not, for the soliloquy which would be his first book of poems.

Nearly everybody is looking for something brave to do. I don't see why people shouldn't write poetry. That's brave. . . .
There is nothing to it but valor and courage.

Outside the cottage the wind through the trees, shaking birches new-spangled in autumn gold, stirred him with an unexpected homesickness. Home—apples, woodpiles, snow, Elliott's grave, the voices of his Derry neighbors.

Valor meant spreading his yellowing sheaf of poems out on the floor of the cottage and finding—or letting the pages reveal—the form they intended to make. There was a kind of unity, a very personal one: the inner and outer weathers of a young poet. Some of his poems didn't fit this plan. The narratives and monologues belonged to a different world; they would have to wait. But the sonnets, ballads, lyrics, laments, going back almost twenty years, were enough for a first book.

He christened his book with a phrase from Longfellow. Then, going to London and following the advice of a policeman, he presented himself and his manuscript to David Nutt, Publisher, Bloomsbury Street. To his astonishment *A Boy's Will* was accepted at once. Published in April 1913, it received many favorable reviews. English readers recognized in the poems, for all their Victorian forms, a hand-hewn honesty and colonial strength which they admired. Overnight the author, thirty-nine years old, famished for attention, became Robert Frost, the poet.

So much, then, for his grandfather's doubts, and for the farmer who said: "Writing is a nice thing to do if you're not well."

Strangers wrote to him, people sought him out, poets came wanting to discuss poetry. In no time he found he had new friends. Ezra Pound (a discoverer of neglected poets) wrote an enthusiastic review for a new magazine in Chicago. Pound took his protégé to meet Yeats. And at the Poetry Bookshop in Kensington, Frost found himself in conversation with more poets than he had ever imagined existed.

England's great gift to Robert Frost was recognition. England discovered him as he was discovering himself. What he had felt for a long time he now could believe was true: that the best of poetry is in some way dramatic, that the sounds of voices carry the deepest meanings, and that words must be as compact as a stone in a shoe.

For Frost, poetry begins in emotion. All the conflicting emotions—cruelty, fear, love, anger, friendship, frustration, tenderness—express themselves in actions, and can be heard in the way voices shape themselves into meanings. In narrative poems the working of will and voice into action is clear enough, but the same, he felt, was true of lyrics and sonnets: they rise up out of past events; they stand lightstruck for an instant; but something is about to happen, if only in mind or mood.

To stage his dramas of human emotions, Frost wanted the settings plain: weather, land, rocks, trees, snow. And he wanted his words plain, just the facts, unadorned. In *A Boy's Will* he had let some poeticisms go into print: "thee" and "thou," "hie me," "bruisèd," "fain," and "list." Never again would he resort to such expedients. As rhyme and meter should take form out of the material of the poem itself (not be imposed on it like some ancient geometry), so the words should arise naturally, taking the reader by eye, ear, nose, even by the hair of his skin:

The buzz saw snarled and rattled in the yard
And made dust and dropped down stove-length sticks of wood,
Sweet-scented stuff when the breeze drew across it.

Or perhaps just conveying sheer animal joy of motion:

You'd think I never had felt before
The weight of an ax-head poised aloft,
The grip on earth of outspread feet,
The life of muscles rocking soft
And smooth and moist in vernal heat.

Many a poet has vowed to have his language simple, but few have succeeded as well as Frost. In his best writing he is able to show or imply the most tangled emotions in words of the plainest sort. Emerson (whom Frost admired) wrote of seeking the language of common speech, but he couldn't resist a loftier diction. In one of his poems Emerson tells of the coming of a snowstorm:

Announced by all the trumpets of the sky
The snow arrives . . .

It is a brilliant brassy line, resonating with the dread and recoil which our race, for more than four glacial ages, has always felt at the shutting in of another winter. But no one can imagine such a line from Frost. No trumpets sound in a December sky; snow does not come down that way.

Nineteen-thirteen was for Robert Frost the watershed year. He had published his first book, learned from it, and was ready to go on. He had found his trail, made good his crossing. His second book would be called *North of Boston*. Frost considered several titles, among them *Farm Servants, New England Hill Folk,* and *New England Eclogues*. All seemed to him a little wrong, consciously bucolic. He wanted only the geographic statement, *North of Boston,* as flat as a map.

The distance between this book and *A Boy's Will* is immense. While there are many fine poems in *A Boy's Will,* the book is clearly a young man's uncertain testament. The poet stands self-consciously before the reader telling of his trials and laments; his rhymes sometimes lapse into singsong, his language into tinted phrases. No such artifice remains in *North of Boston.* Here the poet has departed from the page, leaving it to other people caught midway in some strife. Form does not intrude; rhyme and meter are not imposed as an external shape but move within as surely as a heartbeat. Impulse, thought, words, phrases flow together so that these new poems seem to create themselves before our eyes.

This "quality of dawning" can be seen right from the opening poem, "Mending Wall." At the outset the poem poses a philosophic question about walls. The question is never answered; instead the reader comes upon two neighbors engaged in the ancient business of keeping up boundaries. It seems in this case a silly game or tribal ritual. One man rebuilds the wall because—well, because. The other, half in jest, wants to question what it is they are walling in or walling out. Receiving no sensible reply he nonetheless goes on with the work, balancing one boulder on another until the ceremony is done.

The reader meanwhile is taken in by the action, as though he happened by down the road and cannot help himself. He stops to watch and listen, impelled by that gregarious instinct "to keep together by minding each other's business." He finds himself wondering about walls. But whatever there is to be said about stone walls—and a good deal is said or implied by the two farmers—the reader is left to trudge off saying for himself. The mystery in walls, being unresolved, is undiminished.

North of Boston was accepted for publication in the spring of 1914. By that time Frost was already working on a third book. At the invitation of several friends, he moved his family down to Gloucestershire, to pastoral England, the homeland of so many poets. Pear, cherry, and apple blossoms scented the air, white sheep grazed on the wide hills. A place for talk. His friends were two amateur botanists, a lawyer, and several poets: Rupert Brooke, Walter de la Mare, Wilfrid Gibson, Lascelles Abercrombie, John Drinkwater, Richard Aldington, Ralph Hodgson, Edward Thomas. They imagined, in 1914, that they might live lives of good writing and conversation in the countryside in cottages bearing names like The Old Nailshop and The Gallows.

Brief as their time was, these friends were essential to Frost. He needed to tramp fields again and botanize. Most of all he needed to talk, test his ideas of poetry, listen to the confident young voices of a country which for five hundred years had sustained the highest traditions of writing. Although Frost distrusted all theories but his own (and envied all poets but the dead), nevertheless in many an all-night conversation he found his new friends to be witty and urbane companions. Here in Gloucestershire he found the society of poets he had hoped to find and had not found at Dartmouth or Harvard. And while his friends might disagree with him about Free Verse and Imagism, he needed to hear his own beliefs thrown and drawn and displayed across the tensions of opposing minds.

North of Boston was published but three months before the war began. Generous British people: in the lowery dusk of their imperial century they yet had time to take notice of this raw American visitor and to praise him. New England had shown Frost how to listen to other people; old England helped him to recognize his own voice.

Mending Wall

Something there is that doesn't love a wall,
That sends the frozen-ground-swell under it
And spills the upper boulders in the sun,
And makes gaps even two can pass abreast.
The work of hunters is another thing:
I have come after them and made repair
Where they have left not one stone on a stone,
But they would have the rabbit out of hiding,
To please the yelping dogs. The gaps I mean,
No one has seen them made or heard them made,
But at spring mending-time we find them there.
I let my neighbor know beyond the hill;
And on a day we meet to walk the line
And set the wall between us once again.
We keep the wall between us as we go.
To each the boulders that have fallen to each.
And some are loaves and some so nearly balls
We have to use a spell to make them balance:
"Stay where you are until our backs are turned!"
We wear our fingers rough with handling them.
Oh, just another kind of outdoor game,
One on a side. It comes to little more:
There where it is we do not need the wall:
He is all pine and I am apple orchard.
My apple trees will never get across
And eat the cones under his pines, I tell him.
He only says, "Good fences make good neighbors."
Spring is the mischief in me, and I wonder
If I could put a notion in his head:
"*Why* do they make good neighbors? Isn't it
Where there are cows? But here there are no cows.
Before I built a wall I'd ask to know
What I was walling in or walling out,

And to whom I was like to give offense.
Something there is that doesn't love a wall,
That wants it down." I could say "Elves" to him,
But it's not elves exactly, and I'd rather
He said it for himself. I see him there,
Bringing a stone grasped firmly by the top
In each hand, like an old-stone savage armed.
He moves in darkness as it seems to me,
Not of woods only and the shade of trees.
He will not go behind his father's saying,
And he likes having thought of it so well
He says again, "Good fences make good neighbors."

Putting in the Seed

You come to fetch me from my work tonight
When supper's on the table, and we'll see
If I can leave off burying the white
Soft petals fallen from the apple tree
(Soft petals, yes, but not so barren quite,
Mingled with these, smooth bean and wrinkled pea),
And go along with you ere you lose sight
Of what you came for and become like me,
Slave to a springtime passion for the earth.
How Love burns through the Putting in the Seed
On through the watching for that early birth
When, just as the soil tarnishes with weed,
The sturdy seedling with arched body comes
Shouldering its way and shedding the earth crumbs.

A Leaf-Treader

I have been treading on leaves all day until I am autumn-tired.
God knows all the color and form of leaves I have trodden on and mired.
Perhaps I have put forth too much strength and been too fierce from fear.
I have safely trodden underfoot the leaves of another year.

All summer long they were overhead, more lifted up than I.
To come to their final place in earth they had to pass me by.
All summer long I thought I heard them threatening under their breath.
And when they came it seemed with a will to carry me with them to death.

They spoke to the fugitive in my heart as if it were leaf to leaf.
They tapped at my eyelids and touched my lips with an invitation to grief.
But it was no reason I had to go because they had to go.
Now up, my knee, to keep on top of another year of snow.

The White-Tailed Hornet

The white-tailed hornet lives in a balloon
That floats against the ceiling of the woodshed.
The exit he comes out at like a bullet
Is like the pupil of a pointed gun.
And having power to change his aim in flight,
He comes out more unerring than a bullet.
Verse could be written on the certainty
With which he penetrates my best defense
Of whirling hands and arms about the head
To stab me in the sneeze-nerve of a nostril.
Such is the instinct of it I allow.
Yet how about the insect certainty
That in the neighborhood of home and children
Is such an execrable judge of motives
As not to recognize in me the exception
I like to think I am in everything—
One who would never hang above a bookcase
His Japanese crepe-paper globe for trophy?
He stung me first and stung me afterward.
He rolled me off the field head over heels
And would not listen to my explanations.

That's when I went as visitor to his house.
As visitor at my house he is better.
Hawking for flies about the kitchen door,
In at one door perhaps and out another,
Trust him then not to put you in the wrong.
He won't misunderstand your freest movements.
Let him light on your skin unless you mind
So many prickly grappling feet at once.
He's after the domesticated fly
To feed his thumping grubs as big as he is.
Here he is at his best, but even here—
I watched him where he swooped, he pounced, he struck;

But what he found he had was just a nailhead.
He struck a second time. Another nailhead.
"Those are just nailheads. Those are fastened down."
Then disconcerted and not unannoyed,
He stooped and struck a little huckleberry
The way a player curls around a football.
"Wrong shape, wrong color, and wrong scent," I said.
The huckleberry rolled him on his head.
At last it was a fly. He shot and missed;
And the fly circled round him in derision.
But for the fly he might have made me think
He had been at his poetry, comparing
Nailhead with fly and fly with huckleberry:
How like a fly, how very like a fly.
But the real fly he missed would never do;
The missed fly made me dangerously skeptic.

Won't this whole instinct matter bear revision?
Won't almost any theory bear revision?
To err is human, not to, animal.
Or so we pay the compliment to instinct,
Only too liberal of our compliment
That really takes away instead of gives.
Our worship, humor, conscientiousness
Went long since to the dogs under the table.
And served us right for having instituted
Downward comparisons. As long on earth
As our comparisons were stoutly upward
With gods and angels, we were men at least,
But little lower than the gods and angels.
But once comparisons were yielded downward,
Once we began to see our images
Reflected in the mud and even dust,
'Twas disillusion upon disillusion.
We were lost piecemeal to the animals,
Like people thrown out to delay the wolves.
Nothing but fallibility was left us,
And this day's work made even that seem doubtful.

Design

I found a dimpled spider, fat and white,
On a white heal-all, holding up a moth
Like a white piece of rigid satin cloth—
Assorted characters of death and blight
Mixed ready to begin the morning right,
Like the ingredients of a witches' broth—
A snow-drop spider, a flower like a froth,
And dead wings carried like a paper kite.

What had that flower to do with being white,
The wayside blue and innocent heal-all?
What brought the kindred spider to that height,
Then steered the white moth thither in the night?
What but design of darkness to appall?—
If design govern in a thing so small.

The Objection to Being Stepped On

At the end of the row
I stepped on the toe
Of an unemployed hoe.
It rose in offense
And struck me a blow
In the seat of my sense.
It wasn't to blame
But I called it a name.
And I must say it dealt
Me a blow that I felt
Like malice prepense.
You may call me a fool,
But *was* there a rule
The weapon should be
Turned into a tool?
And what do we see?
The first tool I step on
Turned into a weapon.

The Road Not Taken

Two roads diverged in a yellow wood,
And sorry I could not travel both
And be one traveler, long I stood
And looked down one as far as I could
To where it bent in the undergrowth;

Then took the other, as just as fair,
And having perhaps the better claim,
Because it was grassy and wanted wear;
Though as for that, the passing there
Had worn them really about the same,

And both that morning equally lay
In leaves no step had trodden black.
Oh, I kept the first for another day!
Yet knowing how way leads on to way,
I doubted if I should ever come back.

I shall be telling this with a sigh
Somewhere ages and ages hence:
Two roads diverged in a wood, and I—
I took the one less traveled by,
And that has made all the difference.

The Bonfire

"Oh, let's go up the hill and scare ourselves,
As reckless as the best of them tonight,
By setting fire to all the brush we piled
With pitchy hands to wait for rain or snow.
Oh, let's not wait for rain to make it safe.
The pile is ours: we dragged it bough on bough
Down dark converging paths between the pines.
Let's not care what we do with it tonight.
Divide it? No! But burn it as one pile
The way we piled it. And let's be the talk
Of people brought to windows by a light
Thrown from somewhere against their wallpaper.
Rouse them all, both the free and not so free
With saying what they'd like to do to us
For what they'd better wait till we have done.
Let's all but bring to life this old volcano,
If that is what the mountain ever was—
And scare ourselves. Let wild fire loose we will——"

"And scare you too?" the children said together.

"Why wouldn't it scare me to have a fire
Begin in smudge with ropy smoke, and know
That still, if I repent, I may recall it,
But in a moment not: a little spurt
Of burning fatness, and then nothing but
The fire itself can put it out, and that
By burning out, and before it burns out
It will have roared first and mixed sparks with stars,
And sweeping round it with a flaming sword,
Made the dim trees stand back in wider circle—
Done so much and I know not how much more
I mean it shall not do if I can bind it.
Well if it doesn't with its draft bring on

A wind to blow in earnest from some quarter,
As once it did with me upon an April.
The breezes were so spent with winter blowing
They seemed to fail the bluebirds under them
Short of the perch their languid flight was toward;
And my flame made a pinnacle to heaven
As I walked once around it in possession.
But the wind out-of-doors—you know the saying.
There came a gust. (You used to think the trees
Made wind by fanning, since you never knew
It blow but that you saw the trees in motion.)
Something or someone watching made that gust.
It put the flame tip-down and dabbed the grass
Of over-winter with the least tip-touch
Your tongue gives salt or sugar in your hand.
The place it reached to blackened instantly.
The black was almost all there was by daylight,
That and the merest curl of cigarette smoke—
And a flame slender as the hepaticas,
Bloodroot, and violets so soon to be now.
But the black spread like black death on the ground,
And I think the sky darkened with a cloud
Like winter and evening coming on together.
There were enough things to be thought of then.
Where the field stretches toward the north
And setting sun to Hyla brook, I gave it
To flames without twice thinking, where it verges
Upon the road, to flames too, though in fear
They might find fuel there, in withered brake,
Grass its full length, old silver goldenrod,
And alder and grape vine entanglement,
To leap the dusty deadline. For my own
I took what front there was beside. I knelt
And thrust hands in and held my face away.
Fight such a fire by rubbing not by beating.
A board is the best weapon if you have it.
I had my coat. And oh, I knew, I knew,
And said out loud, I couldn't bide the smother
And heat so close in; but the thought of all
The woods and town on fire by me, and all
The town turned out to fight for me—that held me.
I trusted the brook barrier, but feared
The road would fail; and on that side the fire
Died not without a noise of crackling wood—

Of something more than tinder-grass and weed—
That brought me to my feet to hold it back
By leaning back myself, as if the reins
Were round my neck and I was at the plow.
I won! But I'm sure no one ever spread
Another color over a tenth the space
That I spread coal-black over in the time
It took me. Neighbors coming home from town
Couldn't believe that so much black had come there
While they had backs turned, that it hadn't been there
When they had passed an hour or so before
Going the other way and they not seen it.
They looked about for someone to have done it.
But there was no one. I was somewhere wondering
Where all my weariness had gone and why
I walked so light on air in heavy shoes
In spite of a scorched Fourth-of-July feeling.
Why wouldn't I be scared remembering that?"

"If it scares you, what will it do to us?"

"Scare you. But if you shrink from being scared,
What would you say to war if it should come?
That's what for reasons I should like to know—
If you can comfort me by any answer."

"Oh, but war's not for children—it's for men."

"Now we are digging almost down to China.
My dears, my dears, you thought that—we all thought it.
So your mistake was ours. Haven't you heard, though,
About the ships where war has found them out
At sea, about the towns where war has come
Through opening clouds at night with droning speed
Further o'erhead than all but stars and angels—
And children in the ships and in the towns?
Haven't you heard what we have lived to learn?
Nothing so new—something we had forgotten:
War is for everyone, for children too.
I wasn't going to tell you and I mustn't.
The best way is to come uphill with me
And have our fire and laugh and be afraid."

. . . I seem to want my mountains wild;
The way the wiry gang-boss liked the logjam.
After he'd picked the lock and got it started,
He dodged a log that lifted like an arm
Against the sky to break his back for him,
Then came in dancing, skipping with his life
Across the roar and chaos, and the words
We saw him say along the zigzag journey
Were doubtless as the words we heard him say
On coming nearer: "Wasn't she an *i*-deal
Son-of-a-bitch? You bet she was an *i*-deal."

7. *Franconia*

One by one he saw his friends going off to war, taking jobs in London, disappearing into uniform, vanishing. (Rupert Brooke and Edward Thomas would die in the war.) War tempted Frost, of course—but, he was American, and the father of four children. In February 1915, the Frosts embarked again to cross the western ocean.

So to begin once more. When the Frosts arrived in New York City, Robert had a little money but no job. However, at a newsstand near Grand Central Station he found his name displayed on the cover of a literary magazine; inside, there were two pages reviewing the American edition of *North of Boston*. He was, it appeared, the new New England poet, something of a celebrity already. Well and good, he would pack his family off north and stay to enjoy his fame in New York and Boston; he might even twist the noses of a few editors who for all these years had scoffed him off as a rhymester from the backwoods of somewhere north of Boston.

Robert and Elinor knew exactly where they wanted to settle: in that broad sunny valley beyond the Franconia Mountains or among the neighboring hill farms, where for two summers a local farmer had given them such welcome relief from the hay-fever season in Derry.

I saw this Franconia farm, and it was just what I wanted. . . . So I went up to the farmer and told him I was thinking of moving him to a larger place up the road a piece.

The farmer couldn't see how I was going to do that, because he wasn't interested in selling. I offered him one thousand dollars, with no money down, and told him he could get the larger farm, which he needed, for three thousand dollars, no money down. He finally accepted, only to come to me a day later and said he felt he should get eleven hundred dollars for his farm. I agreed, with no money down.

The transaction didn't happen exactly that way but that is how Frost liked to tell it. There was a mythmaker in him equal to almost any occasion.

The little farm backed up to the foot of Sugar Hill, from which it looked out upon fields where a stream meandered north under curling banks of snow. Beyond the fields and a ramp of foothills the snow rose steeply through hardwood forests, to the cliffs and ravines and the white crest of Mount Lafayette. North of the farm a mile or two by packed road was Franconia village. All the civilization anyone could need was to be found here: a general store, a good library, and an excellent school for the children. The farm itself wasn't much of a farm— just a small house and barn, a garden plot, pasture for a couple of cows, and woods to walk in. It was big enough. Frost was a poet, not a farmer. If people down in the cities made him out to be a farmer-poet, that was all right too. He liked the image of work and play going hand in hand in public: the plainspoken humorous poet, the sturdy practical man of the soil. That was what people believed; that was what sold poems; and that in part was what he was.

The isolation of the farm gave him time to write. Mornings were for sleep and reading, afternoons for walking in the woods. (There was something special in the companionship of trees; even without leaves their conversation was always good, sure to deal with great perplexities: time, seasons, leaving, staying, transience, permanence.) Evenings were for reading to the children, or talk with friends who stopped by to be sociable and enjoy the latest gossip. Frost loved such talk: all the life of the neighborhood eventually came to the surface. As gossip was the lifeblood flowing through the community, so it was for him often the first blush of a poem.

Gossip is what I call guessing at each other. What is he doing? Why? It's man's greatest enterprise, wondering about his world, about himself. . . .

Late at night, when his friends were gone and his family abed, he could sit alone beside the tall woodstove and write. Darkness was his best light: then words seemed to come smiling out of the shadows seeking his company.

. . . What's he up to? Why did I do that? What's behind it? Big It? Little it?

In most respects Franconia's sweeping valley was an ideal location for a poet with a reflective turn of mind and a naturalist's wonder about man's place among the infinities. Nowhere in New England is there a clearer showing of the claw marks of that arctic glacier; nowhere do the seasons succeed each other with more suddenness and pure light.

In Derry he had seen the aftermaths, not only in glacial rubble but in trying to farm when there was almost nothing left of New England farming except the human spirit to keep on. In Franconia it was as though he could step back a hundred and fifty years and meet those rugged people who, in the 1760s, had pushed north through the wild notch and come down to clear this intervale for farming. Farming had never been easy in the north country. Having little to begin with, Franconia people had little to lose to Ohio or California; they took the tourists' dollars as they could, but they never gave up the right to carry their shoulders a little skew-gee if they liked.

My country . . . is milk and sugar country. We get what runs from trees and what runs from cows. You can't do much real farming, for we have a frost every month of the year. You know, the White Mountain farmers say we have nine months of winter and three months of late-in-the-fall! . . .

Chores beginning at 4:30 in the morning, ending long after dark; work in the woods in winter, in the hayfields in summer (with perhaps a cash crop from the summer hotels up on Sugar Hill); sixty years of it more or less for men, sixty-five or seventy for the women. Many sons and daughters had departed to better themselves out west, or gone to learn money jobs in the cities; these people remained. They kept to the old ways of Town Meetings, church suppers, Memorial Day and Fourth of July celebrations, Thanksgivings. In between, they entertained themselves with the eccentricities of the neighbors.

Frost wrote about such people not because they were better than other people—the raw material was the same everywhere—but because rural life was simpler, plainer to see. All the range and variety, intensity and subtlety of human emotions were here. He could see them in the mute longings of children, in the terrible wastage of stifled women. New England was thought by outsiders to "build character." It didn't. It broke your back. You had to have character (or money from elsewhere) to survive.

Down in the cities life was blurred by comforts and "considerations." But there were zones for life, there were limits. In Franconia, in one morning, Frost could walk through all there was of local history: up out of working farms and pastures into woodlots cut over for the third or fourth time, up over talus and ledges to stunted spruce as thick as boulders, finally up to wind-swept crags a mile high where in twelve thousand years not even sedges or moss had yet gained a footing.

Frost was at work on a new book. Poems from Derry were still maturing, some from England were almost ready. He had never succeeded in larruping a poem as one might a horse to make it go. Poems had to come to him in their own ways:

A poem begins with a lump in the throat; a home-sickness or a love-sickness. It is a reaching-out toward expression; an effort to find fulfillment. A complete poem is where an emotion has found its thought and the thought has found the words.

Some poems took years to find their words. Among the slow-growers was "Birches." The impulse for "Birches" had been with him from earliest memories in Lawrence, never changing, always nagging him with the sensations of striving and balance, but always incomplete. Throughout Derry the poem seemed to be waiting a revelation. In England (where no boys swing birches) Frost found the physical act carried through to a spiritual meaning, something to do with earth and human aspirations. Now, in Franconia, after three full decades, the poem found its thought and the thought worked out its words.

There were other times when words came bubbling like a spring runoff. At such times Frost would often write straight through the night. One spring night a few years later he found the cantankerous drafts of a long satiric poem suddenly turned agreeable, almost doing the writing for him. During five hours he hurried to keep up—images, stories, history, snatches of conversation, phrases flowing together as though following some unseen channel. The poem ran on page after page without serious hindrance right to the concluding ironies. Only then did he look up. Dawn's first graying had begun outside his window; across the road the angular rooflines of a barn were emerging. He realized how tired he was, let out completely.

He got up to make coffee. Opening the door, he watched the light coming and listened to the birds waking up in the trees. . . . Suddenly he knew he had company: in that tranquil moment a new troupe of words began to play through his mind:

Whose woods these are I think I know. . . .

Pine trees, dusk, December, a horse-drawn sleigh, falling snow—where did these words come from, so unbidden, so self-assured?

> His house is in the village, though;
> He will not see me stopping here
> To watch his woods fill up with snow.

Derry again, never-to-be-forgotten Derry. The words drifted down out of dark memories: a Christmas Eve when, much too late to be selling anything, he had driven into town to peddle milk and eggs in order to buy presents—no one interested, all busy with their own family celebrations—returning home empty-handed. And yet this poem seemed bent on avoiding the personal reality in order to create a new reality of its own. To make matters more difficult the lyric demanded a tighter than usual bonding of rhyme: four rhymes instead of two, and a linking of one stanza to the next: a-a-b-a, b-b-c-b, c-c-d-c . . .

This posed an enormous challenge: how to keep such a linkage going. Dante could manage a rhyme-chain in Italian, but in English the weight of crude links usually buried its poem. Frost felt the bind at once. Four times he tried to get into his second stanza; four times the lines collapsed. Going on to explore the third stanza, he had better luck.

> He gives his harness bells a shake
> To ask if there is some mistake. . . .

Beginning with the right words, the third stanza not only moved freely to completion but showed the poet how to go back and remake the second.

One other test remained: the ending; where and how to cut the rhyme-chain. Leave it dangling? Stop the poem in a final three rhymes? Jam the end with five rhymes? Try to hook the last link back into the first stanza? All were unworthy of the symmetry the poem had promised itself.

Frost tried one line, then another; both were wrong. But half-hidden in the words of the second attempt—"that bid me on, and there are miles"—he saw the shining ending he had been looking for.

The collaboration was done, the unexpected company satisfied. Groggy but elated, Frost could now go to bed. The sun was just coming up.

"Stopping by Woods on a Snowy Evening" is a work of pure sorcery. Whatever there is about good poetry—a mystery beyond meter, rhymes, images, metaphor—it throws a spell over the simple scene. An experience of pain and humiliation is wholly transformed. Poet, reader, light, dark, duty, life, love join in an instant of communion. No words or rhythms interrupt the spell. They all move in a planetary harmony. Form and energy become one within the poem, as elemental as the mystery of an atom. The poem is a culminating display of why Frost trusted form.

Stopping by Woods on a Snowy Evening

Whose woods these are I think I know.
His house is in the village, though;
He will not see me stopping here
To watch his woods fill up with snow.

My little horse must think it queer
To stop without a farmhouse near
Between the woods and frozen lake
The darkest evening of the year.

He gives his harness bells a shake
To ask if there is some mistake.
The only other sound's the sweep
Of easy wind and downy flake.

The woods are lovely, dark, and deep,
But I have promises to keep,
And miles to go before I sleep,
And miles to go before I sleep.

The Investment

Over back where they speak of life as staying
("You couldn't call it living, for it ain't"),
There was an old, old house renewed with paint,
And in it a piano loudly playing.

Out in the plowed ground in the cold a digger,
Among unearthed potatoes standing still,
Was counting winter dinners, one a hill,
With half an ear to the piano's vigor.

All that piano and new paint back there,
Was it some money suddenly come into?
Or some extravagance young love had been to?
Or old love on an impulse not to care—

Not to sink under being man and wife,
But get some color and music out of life?

The Fear

A lantern-light from deeper in the barn
Shone on a man and woman in the door
And threw their lurching shadows on a house
Nearby, all dark in every glossy window.
A horse's hoof pawed once the hollow floor,
And the back of the gig they stood beside
Moved in a little. The man grasped a wheel.
The woman spoke out sharply, "Whoa, stand still!—
I saw it just as plain as a white plate,"
She said, "as the light on the dashboard ran
Along the bushes at the roadside—a man's face.
You *must* have seen it too."

                                        "I didn't see it.
Are you sure——"

                        "Yes, I'm sure!"

                                        "—it was a face?"

"Joel, I'll have to look. I can't go in,
I can't, and leave a thing like that unsettled.
Doors locked and curtains drawn will make no difference.
I always have felt strange when we came home
To the dark house after so long an absence,
And the key rattled loudly into place
Seemed to warn someone to be getting out
At one door as we entered at another.
What if I'm right, and someone all the time—
Don't hold my arm!"

                        "I say it's someone passing."

"You speak as if this were a traveled road.
You forget where we are. What is beyond
That he'd be going to or coming from

At such an hour of night, and on foot too?
What was he standing still for in the bushes?"

"It's not so very late—it's only dark.
There's more in it than you're inclined to say.
Did he look like——?"

                        "He looked like anyone.
I'll never rest tonight unless I know.
Give me the lantern."

                        "You don't want the lantern."

She pushed past him and got it for herself.

"You're not to come," she said. "This is my business.
If the time's come to face it, I'm the one
To put it the right way. He'd never dare—
Listen! He kicked a stone. Hear that, hear that!
He's coming towards us. Joel, *go* in—please.
Hark!—I don't hear him now. But please go in."

"In the first place you can't make me believe it's——"

"It is—or someone else he's sent to watch.
And now's the time to have it out with him
While we know definitely where he is.
Let him get off and he'll be everywhere
Around us, looking out of trees and bushes
Till I shan't dare to set a foot outdoors.
And I can't stand it. Joel, let me go!"

"But it's nonsense to think he'd care enough."

"You mean you couldn't understand his caring.
Oh, but you see he hadn't had enough—
Joel, I won't—I won't—I promise you.
We mustn't say hard things. You mustn't either."

"I'll be the one, if anybody goes!
But you give him the advantage with this light.
What couldn't he do to us standing here!
And if to see was what he wanted, why,
He has seen all there was to see and gone."

He appeared to forget to keep his hold,
But advanced with her as she crossed the grass.

"What do you want?" she cried to all the dark.

110

She stretched up tall to overlook the light
That hung in both hands, hot against her skirt.

"There's no one; so you're wrong," he said.

                                 "There is.—
What do you want?" she cried, and then herself
Was startled when an answer really came.

"Nothing." It came from well along the road.

She reached a hand to Joel for support:
The smell of scorching woolen made her faint.
"What are you doing round this house at night?"

"Nothing." A pause: there seemed no more to say.

And then the voice again: "You seem afraid.
I saw by the way you whipped up the horse.
I'll just come forward in the lantern-light
And let you see."

                       "Yes, do.—Joel, go back!"

She stood her ground against the noisy steps
That came on, but her body rocked a little.

"You see," the voice said.

                       "Oh." She looked and looked.

"You don't see—I've a child here by the hand.
A robber wouldn't have his family with him."

"What's a child doing at this time of night——?"

"Out walking. Every child should have the memory
Of at least one long-after-bedtime walk.
What, son?"

                "Then I should think you'd try to find
Somewhere to walk——"

                     "The highway, as it happens—
We're stopping for the fortnight down at Dean's."

"But if that's all—Joel—you realize—
You won't think anything. You understand?
You understand that we have to be careful.
This is a very, very lonely place.—
Joel!" She spoke as if she couldn't turn.
The swinging lantern lengthened to the ground,
It touched, it struck, it clattered and went out.

A Servant to Servants

I didn't make you know how glad I was
To have you come and camp here on our land.
I promised myself to get down some day
And see the way you lived, but I don't know!
With a houseful of hungry men to feed
I guess you'd find. . . . It seems to me
I can't express my feelings, any more
Than I can raise my voice or want to lift
My hand (oh, I can lift it when I have to).
Did ever you feel so? I hope you never.
It's got so I don't even know for sure
Whether I *am* glad, sorry, or anything.
There's nothing but a voice-like left inside
That seems to tell me how I ought to feel,
And would feel if I wasn't all gone wrong.
You take the lake. I look and look at it.
I see it's a fair, pretty sheet of water.
I stand and make myself repeat out loud
The advantages it has, so long and narrow,
Like a deep piece of some old running river
Cut short off at both ends. It lies five miles
Straightaway through the mountain notch
From the sink window where I wash the plates,
And all our storms come up toward the house,
Drawing the slow waves whiter and whiter and whiter.
It took my mind off doughnuts and soda biscuit
To step outdoors and take the water dazzle
A sunny morning, or take the rising wind
About my face and body and through my wrapper,
When a storm threatened from the Dragon's Den,
And a cold chill shivered across the lake.
I see it's a fair, pretty sheet of water,
Our Willoughby! How did you hear of it?

I expect, though, everyone's heard of it.
In a book about ferns? Listen to that!
You let things more like feathers regulate
Your going and coming. And you like it here?
I can see how you might. But I don't know!
It would be different if more people came,
For then there would be business. As it is,
The cottages Len built, sometimes we rent them,
Sometimes we don't. We've a good piece of shore
That ought to be worth something, and may yet.
But I don't count on it as much as Len.
He looks on the bright side of everything,
Including me. He thinks I'll be all right
With doctoring. But it's not medicine—
Lowe is the only doctor's dared to say so—
It's rest I want—there, I have said it out—
From cooking meals for hungry hired men
And washing dishes after them—from doing
Things over and over that just won't stay done.
By good rights I ought not to have so much
Put on me, but there seems no other way.
Len says one steady pull more ought to do it.
He says the best way out is always through.
And I agree to that, or in so far
As that I can see no way out but through—
Leastways for me—and then they'll be convinced.
It's not that Len don't want the best for me.
It was his plan our moving over in
Beside the lake from where that day I showed you
We used to live—ten miles from anywhere.
We didn't change without some sacrifice,
But Len went at it to make up the loss.
His work's a man's, of course, from sun to sun,
But he works when he works as hard as I do—
Though there's small profit in comparisons.
(Women and men will make them all the same.)
But work ain't all. Len undertakes too much.
He's into everything in town. This year
It's highways, and he's got too many men
Around him to look after that make waste.
They take advantage of him shamefully,
And proud, too, of themselves for doing so.
We have four here to board, great good-for-nothings,
Sprawling about the kitchen with their talk

While I fry their bacon. Much they care!
No more put out in what they do or say
Than if I wasn't in the room at all.
Coming and going all the time, they are:
I don't learn what their names are, let alone
Their characters, or whether they are safe
To have inside the house with doors unlocked.
I'm not afraid of them, though, if they're not
Afraid of me. There's two can play at that.
I have my fancies: it runs in the family.
My father's brother wasn't right. They kept him
Locked up for years back there at the old farm.
I've been away once—yes, I've been away.
The State Asylum. I was prejudiced;
I wouldn't have sent anyone of mine there;
You know the old idea—the only asylum
Was the poorhouse, and those who could afford,
Rather than send their folks to such a place,
Kept them at home; and it does seem more human.
But it's not so: the place is the asylum.
There they have every means proper to do with,
And you aren't darkening other people's lives—
Worse than no good to them, and they no good
To you in your condition; you can't know
Affection or the want of it in that state.
I've heard too much of the old-fashioned way.
My father's brother, he went mad quite young.
Some thought he had been bitten by a dog,
Because his violence took on the form
Of carrying his pillow in his teeth;
But it's more likely he was crossed in love,
Or so the story goes. It was some girl.
Anyway all he talked about was love.
They soon saw he would do someone a mischief
If he wa'n't kept strict watch of, and it ended
In father's building him a sort of cage,
Or room within a room, of hickory poles,
Like stanchions in the barn, from floor to ceiling—
A narrow passage all the way around.
Anything they put in for furniture
He'd tear to pieces, even a bed to lie on.
So they made the place comfortable with straw,
Like a beast's stall, to ease their consciences.
Of course they had to feed him without dishes.

They tried to keep him clothed, but he paraded
With his clothes on his arm—all of his clothes.
Cruel—it sounds. I s'pose they did the best
They knew. And just when he was at the height,
Father and mother married, and mother came,
A bride, to help take care of such a creature,
And accommodate her young life to his.
That was what marrying father meant to her.
She had to lie and hear love things made dreadful
By his shouts in the night. He'd shout and shout
Until the strength was shouted out of him,
And his voice died down slowly from exhaustion.
He'd pull his bars apart like bow and bowstring,
And let them go and make them twang, until
His hands had worn them smooth as any oxbow.
And then he'd crow as if he thought that child's play—
The only fun he had. I've heard them say, though,
They found a way to put a stop to it.
He was before my time—I never saw him;
But the pen stayed exactly as it was,
There in the upper chamber in the ell,
A sort of catchall full of attic clutter.
I often think of the smooth hickory bars.
It got so I would say—you know, half fooling—
"It's time I took my turn upstairs in jail"—
Just as you will till it becomes a habit.
No wonder I was glad to get away.
Mind you, I waited till Len said the word.
I didn't want the blame if things went wrong.
I was glad though, no end, when we moved out,
And I looked to be happy, and I was,
As I said, for a while—but I don't know!
Somehow the change wore out like a prescription.
And there's more to it than just window views
And living by a lake. I'm past such help—
Unless Len took the notion, which he won't,
And I won't ask him—it's not sure enough.
I s'pose I've got to go the road I'm going:
Other folks have to, and why shouldn't I?
I almost think if I could do like you,
Drop everything and live out on the ground—
But it might be, come night, I shouldn't like it,
Or a long rain. I should soon get enough,
And be glad of a good roof overhead.

I've lain awake thinking of you, I'll warrant,
More than you have yourself, some of these nights.
The wonder was the tents weren't snatched away
From over you as you lay in your beds.
I haven't courage for a risk like that.
Bless you, of course you're keeping me from work,
But the thing of it is, I need to *be* kept.
There's work enough to do—there's always that;
But behind's behind. The worst that you can do
Is set me back a little more behind.
I shan't catch up in this world, anyway.
I'd *rather* you'd not go unless you must.

Birches

When I see birches bend to left and right
Across the lines of straighter darker trees,
I like to think some boy's been swinging them.
But swinging doesn't bend them down to stay
As ice storms do. Often you must have seen them
Loaded with ice a sunny winter morning
After a rain. They click upon themselves
As the breeze rises, and turn many-colored
As the stir cracks and crazes their enamel.
Soon the sun's warmth makes them shed crystal shells
Shattering and avalanching on the snow crust—
Such heaps of broken glass to sweep away
You'd think the inner dome of heaven had fallen.
They are dragged to the withered bracken by the load,
And they seem not to break; though once they are bowed
So low for long, they never right themselves:
You may see their trunks arching in the woods
Years afterwards, trailing their leaves on the ground
Like girls on hands and knees that throw their hair
Before them over their heads to dry in the sun.
But I was going to say when Truth broke in
With all her matter of fact about the ice storm,
I should prefer to have some boy bend them
As he went out and in to fetch the cows—
Some boy too far from town to learn baseball,
Whose only play was what he found himself,
Summer or winter, and could play alone.
One by one he subdued his father's trees
By riding them down over and over again
Until he took the stiffness out of them,
And not one but hung limp, not one was left
For him to conquer. He learned all there was
To learn about not launching out too soon
And so not carrying the tree away

Clear to the ground. He always kept his poise
To the top branches, climbing carefully
With the same pains you use to fill a cup
Up to the brim, and even above the brim.
Then he flung outward, feet first, with a swish,
Kicking his way down through the air to the ground.
So was I once myself a swinger of birches.
And so I dream of going back to be.
It's when I'm weary of considerations,
And life is too much like a pathless wood
Where your face burns and tickles with the cobwebs
Broken across it, and one eye is weeping
From a twig's having lashed across it open.
I'd like to get away from earth awhile
And then come back to it and begin over.
May no fate willfully misunderstand me
And half grant what I wish and snatch me away
Not to return. Earth's the right place for love:
I don't know where it's likely to go better.
I'd like to go by climbing a birch tree,
And climb black branches up a snow-white trunk
Toward heaven, till the tree could bear no more,
But dipped its top and set me down again.
That would be good both going and coming back.
One could do worse than be a swinger of birches.

. . . it is time, strength, tone, light, life, and love—
And even substance lapsing unsubstantial;
The universal cataract of death
That spends to nothingness—and unresisted,
Save by some strange resistance in itself . . .

8. *Poet-in-Residence At Large*

The Franconia poems, entitled *Mountain Interval* and published in 1916, reaffirmed for Americans the reputation Frost had earned among the English. Here was a new voice rising unexpectedly from the hardscrabble farms and swaybacked homes of New England. It was not particularly a New England voice; it was American, following a procession of explorers and settlers, and stopping to give thanks at the sources of the American spirit. These were our watering places, according to Frost: self-reliance, self-government, the courage to go ahead alone if need be, and humility and humor under God's sky. These were our mountain springs, still sustaining us on the height of land, as he believed, of all human experience.

London critics had first caught the unusual timbre of that voice; Frost's poems had "a clear strangeness" and "a deep mysterious tenderness." What was clear was in his language; what was strange was in the drama he found in deceptively plain lives. In the mysterious way of poetry Frost honored his countrymen by showing them the depths of their everyday lives, the verse-sounds in their everyday talk.

Success brought immediate rewards: invitations to lecture or read at several universities, and an offer, by President Alexander Meiklejohn of Amherst, of a teaching position—as Poet-in-Residence—at that college. Frost knew he could teach, lecturing intrigued and appalled him; he accepted both and embarked on two new careers which would grow and sustain him to the end of his life.

He especially welcomed the invitation to come to Amherst. No Athens perhaps, Amherst nevertheless was a fine small college where he could mingle with good minds in a marketplace of ideas. Furthermore, he had his family to think about. He and Elinor were getting on; he was forty-two years old and the children were rapidly growing up. He needed to find a steady income in order to provide for them. Lesley, Carol, Irma, Marjorie—all were artistic, interested in writing, sculpture, books, but not one seemed to have any practical sense; off they went in all directions, following their naïve notions. Living in a college town would give the children time for playfulness and growth.

Frost's idea of teaching was decidedly old-fashioned:

What is a man but all his connections?

. . . college is a second chance to learn to read.

There is the widest choice of companions you will fall in step with, be they living or dead.

Once he had declared that American colleges had invented "the worst system that ever endangered a nation's literature." At Pinkerton Academy and later at Plymouth he had learned the system, then subverted it in favor of his own.

. . . it is the essence of the symposiums I'm after. Heaps of ideas . . . , [r]ooms full of students who want to talk and talk . . . and spill out ideas, to suggest things to me I never thought of.

I don't want to analyze authors. I want to enjoy them, to know them. . . . Youth, I believe, should not analyze its enjoyments. It should live. . . . Criticism is the province of age, not of youth. They'll get to that soon enough.

I am for a wide-open educational system for the free-born. The slaves are another question. . . . I favor the student who will convert my claim on him to his claim on me.

In inviting Frost, it was as though President Meiklejohn had sent all the way to Macedonia for the man who had instructed young Alexander. Poetics, ethics, politics, government: these were proper subjects for young people to explore. Morning classes turned into afternoon discourses beside the football field, and often into late-night rambles along the leafy streets of Amherst, among history, physics, metaphysics, philosophy, tragedy.

Like Aristotle, Frost brought to his symposia a lively interest in knowledge of all sorts, not the least of which was his admiration for scientists. Frost read about science, but more, he absorbed it, converted it into the connective tissue of thought. He envied the scientists venturing off into the unknown. He saw no conflict between science and poetry. They were but two ways of looking at the mystery of life: as "science is the dash of the spirit into the material," so poetry is the dawning of the material into spirit.

Think of the great abysses opened up by our study of the atom. Think of the strange and unaccountable actions of the hurrying winds experienced by our travelers of the skies. Think of the marvels of marine life lately brought to us by the explorers of the distant oceans, each more wonderfully wrought than ever mermaid or water sprite of which the poets dreamed. . . .
. . . I am so sure that it is not given to man to be omniscient. There will always be something left to know, something left to excite the imagination of the poet and those attuned to the great world in which they live.

Two years at Amherst led to other teaching offers. The University of Michigan wanted him, and Harvard and Dartmouth, Florida, Indiana, California. He accepted them all, but always on his own terms. Of course it tickled Frost's sense of the absurd to find famous universities vying for him, this farmer-poet who had never finished college; but if he excited young minds, if he made a few "the fool of books," so much the better. Good readers would come to make the larger connections later on.

Frost's third career, that of giving readings and discussions of poetry, "barding around" as he liked to call it, was forced upon him. Always acutely sensitive to what people might be saying about him, or thinking of him, he had hitherto avoided public appearances. But displays of showmanship with words are expected of Poets-in-Residence, and so at Amherst the lectures began. Once again Carl Burell came from the shadows to help Frost find his way. Long long ago, in high school, Carl had introduced his friend to the frontier humor of Mark Twain and Josh Billings. Frost took to their style, especially Twain's mock seriousness and his gift for startling the truth out of hiding by an unexpected twist of logic. In time, with much pain and practice, Frost found his own style and became a performer in a class with Mark Twain.

Frost knew that most Americans had learned in high school to detest poetry and yet continued to suspect they should admire poets even when they couldn't understand them. But here was a poet who spoke a language as matter-of-fact as a dump truck. Ruggedly handsome, having a quick wit and immense vitality, Frost found that with a few amusing words he could settle an audience, surprise them into going anywhere he wanted to take them.

Most folks are poets. If they were not some of us would have no one to read what we write.

I think [we] come to poetry from Mother Goose up—rhymes, meters, wit, insight, cleverness.

The showman in him, a gift from his father, appeared naturally on the platform. He loved to play off the gaiety or seriousness of his poems against the daily nonsense of politicians and educators.

Sometimes people ask me who I'm going to vote for in the next election. I just tell them to read my collected works and then they'll know.

I'm a Democrat, but I haven't been happy since 1896. I often wonder what an honest Republican would look like. There might be one.

Flattering his listeners, entertaining them, teasing them, twisting them, he led them unsuspecting into poetry.

There was a woman in Sparta who said, "Good fences make good neighbors." And one in Florence, too. And one in Burlington. Insight, you see. A kind of wisdom beyond systems. But something we all feel. This kind of wisdom comes in snatches. Glimpses of something more.

A poem intimates something beyond itself. Saying one thing and meaning another; saying one thing in terms of another. It seeks kindred spirits by suggesting something beyond itself.

I write for kindred spirits. "Yes, I see that. I've felt that too."

Poetry was only a small part of the many enterprises of a people or a nation. It couldn't be separated from the rest, and shouldn't be. Everything anyone did, if it was creative, was a solitary act; if it was successful, a social act.

Among our eternal interests were "superstition, science, and gossip." They formed the web of common intentions which held us together; their pull was on every small enterprise, on even so quiet a poem as "Stopping by Woods on a Snowy Evening."

The important questions in our lives are belief questions. The biggest question of all: the God question. We all have to come to grips with our beliefs, our superstitions. They get in every-where. You can't do a thing with a man who doesn't believe anything. Might as well talk to a Unitarian.

I got a letter from a little girl about that one. Looked pretty young, the handwriting. About her beliefs and that poem.

"Whose woods these are I think I know." She said she got that, that the woods must be God's woods, because the whole world belonged to Him. "His house is in the village, though." She said she understood that. His house was the church. Every village has a church.

But she said the next line gave her trouble. "He will not see me stopping here." She said God sees everywhere, so she got confused and gave up. On me, not on God. Seems a reasonable choice. . . .

Thus over many years did Frost engage his listeners, delighting them, bringing them up to poetry through rhymes, meter, wit, insight, cleverness.

Frost was often criticized by fellow poets for wasting his energies and indulging his ego in platform entertainments. But Frost was a creature of seasons. He needed the alternations: teaching—lecturing—writing. And he needed the money: "enough bread for the butter and butter for the bread."

All in good time new books of poetry came along: *New Hampshire* in 1923, *West-Running Brook* in 1928, *A Further Range* in 1936, and so on across the decades to *In the Clearing*, 1962, published but a few months before his death. Eleven books in all and four collected works, which earned him four Pulitzer Prizes and twoscore honorary degrees.

The 1920s were triumphant years for Robert Frost. Blessed he seemed among poets. But the 1930s—the years of the Great Depression—put him on trial. They tested the aging man more severely than Derry ever had. As the Depression broadened and deepened and became worldwide (as voices of demagogues in Europe harried their peoples toward a new world war), Frost's blunt Americanism seemed ages out of date. His traditional symbols of independence and hard work had little to say to Americans who found themselves shockingly interdependent and out of work.

People demanded new ideas, new prophets, social experimentation, a "New Deal." In spite of cold homes and dark factories, the thirties released a remarkable flood of art, drama, and poetry, but Frost had little part in it. He stood athwart the torrent: he didn't like the sound of the New Deal, he distrusted Franklin Roosevelt, and he had no use for the new fashion of Free Verse. Yankee pragmatism should have helped him to hear the strength evident in some of the new verse, but Frost felt assaulted on all sides. He feared the way his country was going, he worried about his children, and he secretly doubted his gifts as a poet.

It is of course an academic argument whether rhyme and meter have anything essential to do with poetry. As Frost saw it, form in poetry was no elegance or artifice, but an affirmation of the laws of order and succession decreed throughout the universe. Not a planet in the sky, not an atom of earth's crust but obeyed absolute laws; not a creature or flower but was granted life according to the strictest jurisdiction. Order meant continuity and sanity; the opposite, chaos.

He had very personal reasons for fearing a loss of Nature's controls. He had seen cancer consume his mother; Elinor was now suffering from cancer. His father had gone down in mania and depression; his sister Jeanie had wasted and died during nine years in a mental hospital. And all too well did he know the irrational primitive abiding within himself.

To make matters more difficult, nothing seemed to work out for his children. For all the love and plans and lands and education he supplied them with, nothing seemed to go right. Artistic they were, but headstrong, undisciplined. His advice went unheeded. All he got back from his children was what he wanted least: mirror flashes of himself, his own contrariness, his own blind groping through early manhood.

In his life, he had been able to steal time, laying it away to good purpose, coming to his first book at an age when most poets are faltering or defunct. But in the lives of his children, time had escaped him. Hard as it was to realize, his children were children no more. All except Marjorie were over thirty, approaching middle age.

Lesley, the oldest, was away, going from job to job, selling books, writing, teaching, unable to settle down. Marriage brought her two children and a divorce. Irma, the second girl, oversensitive and given to hysterical tirades, had fared no better. Beginning in architecture, turning to art, marrying, running away while pregnant, making up. Always a new outburst—there was no telling how that marriage would work out.

The boy, Carol, was a special worry. Carol was a struggling poet, determined to emulate his father. In South Shaftsbury, Vermont, Frost had found him a good farm, shown him how to prune back the apple trees, how to set out red pine seedlings. Carol worked with the intensity of a poet but he lacked the practical sense of a farmer. Finally both Carol and his wife had come down with tuberculosis; Frost had had to settle them on a sheep ranch in California. Convalescence went on and on and on.

Worse was yet to come. Marjorie, the happy one, the uncomplicated one, started off in nursing at Johns Hopkins. After one semester the family weakness asserted itself and she succumbed to tuberculosis. Recovering in Colorado, she fell in love with a Montana rancher. So quick it all happened: Marjorie marrying, joyously going to the hospital to have her first baby, dying of childbed fever.

> A voice said, Look me in the stars
> And tell me truly, men of earth,
> If all the soul-and-body scars
> Were not too much to pay for birth.

Puerperal fever was a terrible trick of fate. It came from carelessness, dirty hands—it entered in chains of cocci through the wound of birth—it bound a young woman at the moment of immortality and held her for fire.

For six weeks Marjorie lay hospitalized in Billings, Montana, while the infection smoldered in her body. In desperation Robert and Elinor had her flown to the Mayo Clinic in Minnesota, where, it was claimed, a new serum sometimes worked. Mercifully in coma, Marjorie lingered yet another week. Just at the end her mind cleared a little.

131

The only way I could reach her was by putting my hand backward and forward between us, as in counting out and saying with over-emphasis "You—and—Me." The last time I did that, the day before she died, she smiled faintly and answered "All the same," frowned slightly and made it "Always the same."

These misfortunes proved too much for Elinor. "I long to die myself," she wrote to a friend. It was not long. In the spring of 1938, in Florida, recuperating from a cancer operation but suffering a recurrence of acute angina, Elinor died.

Carol overcame tuberculosis in the beneficent climate of southern California. Eventually his wife also recovered, although soon afterward she had to be hospitalized for a hysterectomy. But sheep-ranching failed. Carol was not quite a poet and not quite a farmer. At the age of thirty-eight—at that age when his father had had the will to face down all outside demands, uproot his family, go to England and become famous—humiliated, despondent beyond reach, Carol shot himself.

Neither Out Far nor In Deep

The people along the sand
All turn and look one way.
They turn their back on the land.
They look at the sea all day.

As long as it takes to pass
A ship keeps raising its hull;
The wetter ground like glass
Reflects a standing gull.

The land may vary more;
But wherever the truth may be—
The water comes ashore,
And the people look at the sea.

They cannot look out far.
They cannot look in deep.
But when was that ever a bar
To any watch they keep?

Wild Grapes

What tree may not the fig be gathered from?
The grape may not be gathered from the birch?
It's all you know the grape, or know the birch.
As a girl gathered from the birch myself
Equally with my weight in grapes, one autumn,
I ought to know what tree the grape is fruit of.
I was born, I suppose, like anyone,
And grew to be a little boyish girl
My brother could not always leave at home.
But that beginning was wiped out in fear
The day I swung suspended with the grapes,
And was come after like Eurydice
And brought down safely from the upper regions;
And the life I live now's an extra life
I can waste as I please on whom I please.
So if you see me celebrate two birthdays,
And give myself out as two different ages,
One of them five years younger than I look—

One day my brother led me to a glade
Where a white birch he knew of stood alone,
Wearing a thin headdress of pointed leaves,
And heavy on her heavy hair behind,
Against her neck, an ornament of grapes.
Grapes, I knew grapes from having seen them last year.
One bunch of them, and there began to be
Bunches all round me growing in white birches,
The way they grew round Leif the Lucky's German;
Mostly as much beyond my lifted hands, though,
As the moon used to seem when I was younger,
And only freely to be had for climbing.
My brother did the climbing; and at first
Threw me down grapes to miss and scatter
And have to hunt for in sweet fern and hardhack;

Which gave him some time to himself to eat,
But not so much, perhaps, as a boy needed.
So then, to make me wholly self-supporting,
He climbed still higher and bent the tree to earth
And put it in my hands to pick my own grapes.
"Here, take a treetop, I'll get down another.
Hold on with all your might when I let go."
I said I had the tree. It wasn't true.
The opposite was true. The tree had me.
The minute it was left with me alone,
It caught me up as if I were the fish
And it the fishpole. So I was translated,
To loud cries from my brother of "Let go!
Don't you know anything, you girl? Let go!"
But I, with something of the baby grip
Acquired ancestrally in just such trees
When wilder mothers than our wildest now
Hung babies out on branches by the hands
To dry or wash or tan, I don't know which
(You'll have to ask an evolutionist)—
I held on uncomplainingly for life.
My brother tried to make me laugh to help me.
"What are you doing up there in those grapes?
Don't be afraid. A few of them won't hurt you.
I mean, they won't pick you if you don't them."
Much danger of my picking anything!
By that time I was pretty well reduced
To a philosophy of hang-and-let-hang.
"Now you know how it feels," my brother said,
"To be a bunch of fox grapes, as they call them,
That when it thinks it has escaped the fox
By growing where it shouldn't—on a birch,
Where a fox wouldn't think to look for it—
And if he looked and found it, couldn't reach it—
Just then come you and I to gather it.
Only you have the advantage of the grapes
In one way: you have one more stem to cling by,
And promise more resistance to the picker."

One by one I lost off my hat and shoes,
And still I clung. I let my head fall back,
And shut my eyes against the sun, my ears
Against my brother's nonsense. "Drop," he said,
"I'll catch you in my arms. It isn't far."

(Stated in lengths of him it might not be.)
"Drop or I'll shake the tree and shake you down."
Grim silence on my part as I sank lower,
My small wrists stretching till they showed the banjo strings.
"Why, if she isn't serious about it!
Hold tight awhile till I think what to do.
I'll bend the tree down and let you down by it."
I don't know much about the letting down;
But once I felt ground with my stocking feet
And the world came revolving back to me,
I know I looked long at my curled-up fingers,
Before I straightened them and brushed the bark off.
My brother said: "Don't you weigh anything?
Try to weigh something next time, so you won't
Be run off with by birch trees into space."

It wasn't my not weighing anything
So much as my not knowing anything—
My brother had been nearer right before.
I had not taken the first step in knowledge;
I had not learned to let go with the hands,
As still I have not learned to with the heart,
And have no wish to with the heart—nor need,
That I can see. The mind—is not the heart.
I may yet live, as I know others live,
To wish in vain to let go with the mind—
Of cares, at night, to sleep; but nothing tells me
That I need learn to let go with the heart.

Desert Places

Snow falling and night falling fast, oh, fast
In a field I looked into going past,
And the ground almost covered smooth in snow,
But a few weeds and stubble showing last.

The woods around it have it—it is theirs.
All animals are smothered in their lairs.
I am too absent-spirited to count;
The loneliness includes me unawares.

And lonely as it is, that loneliness
Will be more lonely ere it will be less—
A blanker whiteness of benighted snow
With no expression, nothing to express.

They cannot scare me with their empty spaces
Between stars—on stars where no human race is.
I have it in me so much nearer home
To scare myself with my own desert places.

Provide, Provide

The witch that came (the withered hag)
To wash the steps with pail and rag
Was once the beauty Abishag,

The picture pride of Hollywood.
Too many fall from great and good
For you to doubt the likelihood.

Die early and avoid the fate,
Or if predestined to die late,
Make up your mind to die in state.

Make the whole stock exchange your own!
If need be occupy a throne,
Where nobody can call *you* crone.

Some have relied on what they knew,
Others on being simply true.
What worked for them might work for you.

No memory of having starred
Atones for later disregard
Or keeps the end from being hard.

Better to go down dignified
With boughten friendship at your side
Than none at all. Provide, provide!

The Witch of Coös

I stayed the night for shelter at a farm
Behind the mountain, with a mother and son,
Two old-believers. They did all the talking.

MOTHER. Folks think a witch who has familiar spirits
She could call up to pass a winter evening,
But won't, should be burned at the stake or something.
Summoning spirits isn't "Button, button,
Who's got the button," I would have them know.

SON. Mother can make a common table rear
And kick with two legs like an army mule.

MOTHER. And when I've done it, what good have I done?
Rather than tip a table for you, let me
Tell you what Ralle the Sioux Control once told me.
He said the dead had souls, but when I asked him
How could that be—I thought the dead were souls—
He broke my trance. Don't that make you suspicious
That there's something the dead are keeping back?
Yes, there's something the dead are keeping back.

SON. You wouldn't want to tell him what we have
Up attic, mother?

MOTHER.   Bones—a skeleton.

SON. But the headboard of mother's bed is pushed
Against the attic door: the door is nailed.
It's harmless. Mother hears it in the night,
Halting perplexed behind the barrier
Of door and headboard. Where it wants to get
Is back into the cellar where it came from.

MOTHER. We'll never let them, will we, son? We'll never!

SON. It left the cellar forty years ago
And carried itself like a pile of dishes

Up one flight from the cellar to the kitchen,
Another from the kitchen to the bedroom,
Another from the bedroom to the attic,
Right past both father and mother, and neither stopped it.
Father had gone upstairs; mother was downstairs.
I was a baby: I don't know where I was.

MOTHER.   The only fault my husband found with me—
I went to sleep before I went to bed,
Especially in winter when the bed
Might just as well be ice and the clothes snow.
The night the bones came up the cellar stairs
Toffile had gone to bed alone and left me,
But left an open door to cool the room off
So as to sort of turn me out of it.
I was just coming to myself enough
To wonder where the cold was coming from,
When I heard Toffile upstairs in the bedroom
And thought I heard him downstairs in the cellar.
The board we had laid down to walk dry-shod on
When there was water in the cellar in spring
Struck the hard cellar bottom. And then someone
Began the stairs, two footsteps for each step,
The way a man with one leg and a crutch,
Or a little child, comes up. It wasn't Toffile:
It wasn't anyone who could be there.
The bulkhead double doors were double-locked
And swollen tight and buried under snow.
The cellar windows were banked up with sawdust
And swollen tight and buried under snow.
It was the bones. I knew them—and good reason.
My first impulse was to get to the knob
And hold the door. But the bones didn't try
The door; they halted helpless on the landing,
Waiting for things to happen in their favor.
The faintest restless rustling ran all through them.
I never could have done the thing I did
If the wish hadn't been too strong in me
To see how they were mounted for this walk.
I had a vision of them put together
Not like a man, but like a chandelier.
So suddenly I flung the door wide on him.
A moment he stood balancing with emotion,
And all but lost himself. (A tongue of fire

Flashed out and licked along his upper teeth.
Smoke rolled inside the sockets of his eyes.)
Then he came at me with one hand outstretched,
The way he did in life once; but this time
I struck the hand off brittle on the floor,
And fell back from him on the floor myself.
The finger-pieces slid in all directions.
(Where did I see one of those pieces lately?
Hand me my button box—it must be there.)
I sat up on the floor and shouted, "Toffile,
It's coming up to you." It had its choice
Of the door to the cellar or the hall.
It took the hall door for the novelty,
And set off briskly for so slow a thing,
Still going every which way in the joints, though,
So that it looked like lightning or a scribble,
From the slap I had just now given its hand.
I listened till it almost climbed the stairs
From the hall to the only finished bedroom,
Before I got up to do anything;
Then ran and shouted, "Shut the bedroom door,
Toffile, for my sake!" "Company?" he said,
"Don't make me get up; I'm too warm in bed."
So lying forward weakly on the handrail
I pushed myself upstairs, and in the light
(The kitchen had been dark) I had to own
I could see nothing. "Toffile, I don't see it.
It's with us in the room, though. It's the bones."
"What bones?" "The cellar bones—out of the grave."
That made him throw his bare legs out of bed
And sit up by me and take hold of me.
I wanted to put out the light and see
If I could see it, or else mow the room,
With our arms at the level of our knees,
And bring the chalk-pile down. "I'll tell you what—
It's looking for another door to try.
The uncommonly deep snow has made him think
Of his old song, 'The Wild Colonial Boy,'
He always used to sing along the tote road.
He's after an open door to get outdoors.
Let's trap him with an open door up attic."
Toffile agreed to that, and sure enough,
Almost the moment he was given an opening,
The steps began to climb the attic stairs.

I heard them. Toffile didn't seem to hear them.
"Quick!" I slammed to the door and held the knob.
"Toffile, get nails." I made him nail the door shut
And push the headboard of the bed against it.
Then we asked was there anything
Up attic that we'd ever want again.
The attic was less to us than the cellar.
If the bones liked the attic, let them have it.
Let them stay in the attic. When they sometimes
Come down the stairs at night and stand perplexed
Behind the door and headboard of the bed,
Brushing their chalky skull with chalky fingers,
With sounds like the dry rattling of a shutter,
That's what I sit up in the dark to say—
To no one anymore since Toffile died.
Let them stay in the attic since they went there.
I promised Toffile to be cruel to them
For helping them be cruel once to him.

SON.   We think they had a grave down in the cellar.

MOTHER.   We know they had a grave down in the cellar.

SON.   We never could find out whose bones they were.

MOTHER.   Yes, we could too, son. Tell the truth for once.
They were a man's his father killed for me.
I mean a man he killed instead of me.
The least I could do was help dig their grave.
We were about it one night in the cellar.
Son knows the story: but 'twas not for him
To tell the truth, suppose the time had come.
Son looks surprised to see me end a lie
We'd kept up all these years between ourselves
So as to have it ready for outsiders.
But tonight I don't care enough to lie—
I don't remember why I ever cared.
Toffile, if he were here, I don't believe
Could tell you why he ever cared himself. . . .

She hadn't found the finger-bone she wanted
Among the buttons poured out in her lap.
I verified the name next morning: Toffile.
The rural letter box said Toffile Lajway.

Never again would birds' song be the same.
And to do that to birds was why she came.

9. Outer Dark

Robert Frost returned once to Derry, bringing Elinor's ashes. Elinor had wished to be left beside Hyla Brook, whose spring song was still being made over into summer jewelweed. What better place to come to earth than where she had revived after the death of her firstborn? What better place than where Robert had learned to transmute some of his fury into loving "the things we love for what they are"?

But the little farm had been all let go. Elinor's rock garden had reverted to a bank of glacial boulders, the vegetable garden to a blowdown of weeds. The owner of the farm was talking of putting in a filling station, fixing up the barn for a garage. Hyla Brook, it is true, had not changed. It still found its pretty way from the swamp down the rocky promenade into a grove of pines, but Frost had no heart to leave Elinor here among such desolation.

Thirty years. The squabbles with his grandfather, the struggles with himself to get by in farming and live by writing—all to make a few words go together in a few poems. Less than thirty years since he and Elinor had left Derry, years that had used her up, and everything, nearly everything, obliterated but the poems. Perhaps that was what his apprenticeship in New England was all about: poems were preparation. They began in bravado, holding back fear, and ended in fortitude.

Frost understood the calamities which had recently befallen his family and himself. Guilty he was, like Job, of neglect and vainglory. Unlike Job he could find no angel to combat, nor comfort himself with the belief that God had singled him out to make a special exhibition. No God needed to inquire where he was when the foundations of earth were laid down and the stars hung out across the limitless darkness. Perhaps there was no God or design or purpose anywhere in the universe.

Luckily for Frost at this time of need, into his life came a remarkable woman, the wife of a Harvard professor, offering help. As a student at Bryn Mawr, Kathleen Morrison had met Frost during one of his early lecture tours. She had been caught up in his poetry, swept along by his adventuring mind. Now, with little idea of the demands which would be made upon her but with faith in his talent, she volunteered to do what she could, and Frost accepted. Thereafter, Mrs. Morrison became his secretary, scribe, booking agent, real estate consultant, and occasionally his nurse and savior. She found him a permanent home in Cambridge, Massachusetts, a summer farm in Ripton, Vermont; she fended off the curious or idolatrous public, admitted his friends, suffered his eruptions, and helped preserve him for another quarter-century of productive life.

As much for the solace of kindred spirits as for income, he returned to teaching and lecturing. Amherst, Harvard, Dartmouth welcomed him back for whatever time he could spare them, and fall and spring he carried on his tours across the country. In both of these professions he grew better year by year. After a lifetime in literature and history he knew most of the paths to hell, and some of the ways back. What had been a young poet's precocious insight into the sufferings of others deepened into a teacher's mature understanding of himself. Students responded. It was not a "course" they were taking but a presence taking them. (The daily voyages might go anywhere, the discussion might go on all evening, even into dawn.) It was vitality, intensity, insight, excitement over facts and phrases—some glimmering of the ageless spirit of a poet.

He mellowed. The jealousy Frost felt for other poets softened and turned, if not into goodwill, at least into good humor. Indeed, much of what was thought to be malice by serious and sensitive people was only the rough play of his wit. He loved challenging good minds, sparring with them. It was his lot to have his jabs—either in poetry or conversation—taken too seriously. As one of his friends has said: "He was tough, but more than that, he was foxy. And sometimes being foxy is better than being tough."

Whether foxy or tough, sardonic or tender, neither his students nor his public audiences cared. He was all of those and much more to them. Right to his last days Frost could fill a classroom or an auditorium: here was the indestructible old fellow again, white hair in a snowsquall, ice-blue eyes glinting above a granite grin, joking, exaggerating, relishing his play with words, saying his poems and salting them with quips about professors who write in footnotes, or poets who write in cryptograms. For some of his listeners he was the only poet they would ever meet; for many the only poet they would ever remember.

In summer he returned to his cabin in Ripton, where he could write, garden, botanize, and preside as a kind of Jovian spirit (benign or irascible) at the sessions of the Bread Loaf Writers' Conference. The little cabin suited his needs. Furnished mainly with books, it provided a retreat for meditation and writing. When visitors got too thick, or when memories overwhelmed him, he could escape into the woods with his dog, Gillie.

This period in his life was not just a prolonged spell of Indian summer, but a new growing season, a time of good harvests. Five more books of poetry and a final collection appeared. It may well be that Frost did his most original writing in the first six books. After 1940 his poems change in both subject and style. He turns to long philosophic poems, or to short aphoristic statements and conundrums. Drama thins out, becoming a framework for speculation; the speaking voice becomes a thinking voice; rhymes sometimes decline to mere cleverness. Yet it is surprising, season by season, how often the original vitality returns. Some of Frost's best poems come from this final period. At seventy-two he can still summon his resources for a philosophic gathering in "Directive." At eighty-seven he can still go forth into a winter wood and return with the cold lights caught in a crystal lyric.

For a while in the 1950s and early '60s, Frost was attracted by the scintillations of national politics. He accepted an invitation to come to Washington as Consultant in Poetry—later as Consultant in the Humanities—to the Library of Congress. But congressmen don't consult poets, especially one who is as likely to recognize Athens or Carthage in the daily news as Washington or Moscow.

Unfinished business. . . . I'm much in favor of unfinished business. Some [people] aren't, but every single heading in the newspaper represents a whole lot of things that have got to stay unfinished, that can't be finished. Us and Russia, that might take a couple of hundred years before it's finished. That's one of the hard things about dying, wondering how the unfinished business will come out.

He helped to get Ezra Pound released from incarceration in a mental hospital, and he was sent off on goodwill tours to Brazil, England, Israel. But there was little for him to do in Washington. Nor was it in his nature to be a small eccentric planet among the larger satellites revolving about the White House.

In the late summer of 1962 Frost was sent by President Kennedy to Russia, where he met with poets, and, briefly, with Premier Khrushchev. No doubt the two old men liked each other, each one recognizing in the other the toughness of a rural patriot who has lived through times of terror and change. Frost wanted to discuss a favorite subject—the magnanimity which should govern the acts of two great rivals—but Khrushchev was preoccupied with other business. He was, as it later turned out, shipping missiles into Cuba.

Frost returned from Russia with a liking for its poets, and a respect for the spartan regime he had seen there. But his faith in America was still the credo he had held to most of his life:

I would rather [see us] perish as Athens than prevail as Sparta. The tone is Athens. The tone is freedom to the point of destruction. Democracy means all the risks taken—conflict of opinion, conflict of personality, eccentricity. We are Athens, daring to be all sorts of people.

Late in the fall of 1962 (after the unfinished business of the Cuban missile crisis) Robert Frost entered a Boston hospital with an acute flareup of the old man's disease. The prostate operation was successful, he seemed to be well on the way to recovery, but then a series of vascular complications set in which brought him down. He was approaching his eighty-ninth birthday when he died. The nation was nearing its two hundredth.

America, Frost often said, is hard to see: a wide and varied land still realizing westward; a people made up of all people, who, for all their conflicting interests and love of change, still presume freely to govern themselves. What Americans will make of their lands and their freedoms cannot yet be said.

Nor is the past any easier to see. Almost unnoticed the present slips away to join the sediments of the past. Yet among the perplexities left behind for historians—the chipped stone axes, the stone walls and empty cellar holes—the poems of Robert Frost remain as a record of exceptional clarity. Events shaped the lives of his people as their voices shaped these poems. They tell us of our recent selves, such as we were, such as we were becoming.

Fire and Ice

Some say the world will end in fire,
Some say in ice.
From what I've tasted of desire
I hold with those who favor fire.
But if it had to perish twice,
I think I know enough of hate
To say that for destruction ice
Is also great
And would suffice.

To an Ancient

Your claims to immortality were two.
The one you made, the other one you grew.
Sorry to have no name for you but You.

We never knew exactly where to look,
But found one in the delta of a brook,
One in a cavern where you used to cook.

Coming on such an ancient human trace
Seems as expressive of the human race
As meeting someone living, face to face.

We date you by your depth in silt and dust
Your probable brute nature is discussed.
At which point we are totally nonplussed.

You made the eolith, you grew the bone,
The second more peculiarly your own,
And likely to have been enough alone.

You make me ask if I would go to time
Would I gain anything by using rhyme?
Or aren't the bones enough I live to lime?

The Most of It

He thought he kept the universe alone;
For all the voice in answer he could wake
Was but the mocking echo of his own
From some tree-hidden cliff across the lake.
Some morning from the boulder-broken beach
He would cry out on life, that what it wants
Is not its own love back in copy speech,
But counter-love, original response.
And nothing ever came of what he cried
Unless it was the embodiment that crashed
In the cliff's talus on the other side,
And then in the far-distant water splashed,
But after a time allowed for it to swim,
Instead of proving human when it neared
And someone else additional to him,
As a great buck it powerfully appeared,
Pushing the crumpled water up ahead,
And landed pouring like a waterfall,
And stumbled through the rocks with horny tread,
And forced the underbrush—and that was all.

Closed for Good

Much as I own I owe
The passers of the past
Because their to and fro
Has cut this road to last,
I owe them more today
Because they've gone away

And come not back with steed
And chariot to chide
My slowness with their speed
And scare me to one side.
They have found other scenes
For haste and other means.

They leave the road to me
To walk in saying naught
Perhaps but to a tree
Inaudibly in thought,
"From you the road receives
A priming coat of leaves.

"And soon for lack of sun,
The prospects are in white
It will be further done,
But with a coat so light
The shape of leaves will show
Beneath the brush of snow."

And so on into winter
Till even I have ceased
To come as a foot printer,
And only some slight beast
So mousy or so foxy
Shall print there as my proxy.

I Could Give All to Time

To Time it never seems that he is brave
To set himself against the peaks of snow
To lay them level with the running wave,
Nor is he overjoyed when they lie low,
But only grave, contemplative and grave.

What now is inland shall be ocean isle,
Then eddies playing round a sunken reef
Like the curl at the corner of a smile;
And I could share Time's lack of joy or grief
At such a planetary change of style.

I could give all to Time except—except
What I myself have held. But why declare
The things forbidden that while the Customs slept
I have crossed to Safety with? For I am There,
And what I would not part with I have kept.

An Old Man's Winter Night

All out-of-doors looked darkly in at him
Through the thin frost, almost in separate stars,
That gathers on the pane in empty rooms.
What kept his eyes from giving back the gaze
Was the lamp tilted near them in his hand.
What kept him from remembering what it was
That brought him to that creaking room was age.
He stood with barrels round him—at a loss.
And having scared the cellar under him
In clomping here, he scared it once again
In clomping off—and scared the outer night,
Which has its sounds, familiar, like the roar
Of trees and crack of branches, common things,
But nothing so like beating on a box.
A light he was to no one but himself
Where now he sat, concerned with he knew what,
A quiet light, and then not even that.
He consigned to the moon—such as she was,
So late-arising—to the broken moon,
As better than the sun in any case
For such a charge, his snow upon the roof,
His icicles along the wall to keep;
And slept. The log that shifted with a jolt
Once in the stove, disturbed him and he shifted,
And eased his heavy breathing, but still slept.
One aged man—one man—can't keep a house,
A farm, a countryside, or if he can,
It's thus he does it of a winter night.

Come In

As I came to the edge of the woods,
Thrush music—hark!
Now if it was dusk outside,
Inside it was dark.

Too dark in the woods for a bird
By sleight of wing
To better its perch for the night,
Though it still could sing.

The last of the light of the sun
That had died in the west
Still lived for one song more
In a thrush's breast.

Far in the pillared dark
Thrush music went—
Almost like a call to come in
To the dark and lament.

But no, I was out for stars:
I would not come in.
I meant not even if asked,
And I hadn't been.

Directive

Back out of all this now too much for us,
Back in a time made simple by the loss
Of detail, burned, dissolved, and broken off
Like graveyard marble sculpture in the weather,
There is a house that is no more a house
Upon a farm that is no more a farm
And in a town that is no more a town.
The road there, if you'll let a guide direct you
Who only has at heart your getting lost,
May seem as if it should have been a quarry—
Great monolithic knees the former town
Long since gave up pretense of keeping covered.
And there's a story in a book about it:
Besides the wear of iron wagon wheels
The ledges show lines ruled southeast-northwest,
The chisel work of an enormous Glacier
That braced his feet against the Arctic Pole.
You must not mind a certain coolness from him
Still said to haunt this side of Panther Mountain.
Nor need you mind the serial ordeal
Of being watched from forty cellar holes
As if by eye pairs out of forty firkins.
As for the woods' excitement over you
That sends light rustle rushes to their leaves,
Charge that to upstart inexperience.
Where were they all not twenty years ago?
They think too much of having shaded out
A few old pecker-fretted apple trees.
Make yourself up a cheering song of how
Someone's road home from work this once was,
Who may be just ahead of you on foot
Or creaking with a buggy load of grain.
The height of the adventure is the height
Of country where two village cultures faded

Into each other. Both of them are lost.
And if you're lost enough to find yourself
By now, pull in your ladder road behind you
And put a sign up CLOSED to all but me.
Then make yourself at home. The only field
Now left's no bigger than a harness gall.
First there's the children's house of make-believe,
Some shattered dishes underneath a pine,
The playthings in the playhouse of the children.
Weep for what little things could make them glad.
Then for the house that is no more a house,
But only a belilaced cellar hole,
Now slowly closing like a dent in dough.
This was no playhouse but a house in earnest.
Your destination and your destiny's
A brook that was the water of the house,
Cold as a spring as yet so near its source,
Too lofty and original to rage.
(We know the valley streams that when aroused
Will leave their tatters hung on barb and thorn.)
I have kept hidden in the instep arch
Of an old cedar at the waterside
A broken drinking goblet like the Grail
Under a spell so the wrong ones can't find it,
So can't get saved, as Saint Mark says they mustn't.
(I stole the goblet from the children's playhouse.)
Here are your waters and your watering place.
Drink and be whole again beyond confusion.

[In Winter in the Woods...]

In winter in the woods alone
Against the trees I go.
I mark a maple for my own
And lay the maple low.

At four o'clock I shoulder ax,
And in the afterglow
I link a line of shadowy tracks
Across the tinted snow.

I see for Nature no defeat
In one tree's overthrow
Or for myself in my retreat
For yet another blow.

Acknowledgments

Mr. Frost was reticent about the details of his life, playful with myths, and thoroughly aware that he was "a somebody." Therefore the "facts" about him must always be read with some doubt. The standard works on his life, the Lawrance Thompson–R.H. Winnick three-volume biography, Kathleen Morrison's *Robert Frost—A Pictorial Chronicle,* and other studies, were especially helpful in intimating the poet's complex personality.

Interviews with Robert Frost (Holt, Rinehart, and Winston, 1966) edited by Edward Connery Lathem, provided an essential resource. Equally valuable was the stage play, *Swinger of Birches,* compiled from tapes of Mr. Frost's lectures and readings, and written by Terrence Ortwein of the Choate School.

Many people have helped in enlarging and shaping this manuscript. For such generous assistance I am indebted to the poet Philip Booth, to John S. Dickey and Edward Lathem of Dartmouth, to John Pillsbury, Ray Nash, Barbara Haskell, Suzanne Sweet, Jean Robinson, and Ben and Elisabeth Bradley.

Thanks, too, to Alfred C. Edwards, Executor of the Estate of Robert Frost, not only for permission to publish these poems but for many suggestions as well.

Lastly, thanks to Dartmouth College for its exceptional libraries; and to the Amos Tuck School for a quiet room and generous neglect.

—*David Bradley*

I would like to thank my wife, Babs Kavanaugh, for her love and support during this project; Ralph Steiner for his invaluable friendship and guidance; the Foxes, the Bradleys, the Dupuys, the Campions, and all the other fine people who are such a part of my New England experience. Further let me thank the National Geographic Society for permission to reprint the photographs on pages 28, 30, and 102; and finally Al Edwards not only for his support but for sharing with me his great respect and love for Robert Frost.

—*Dewitt Jones*